मानसशास्त्राच्या सर्व विद्यार्थ्यांसाठी व स्पर्धापरीक्षांसाठी उपयुक्त

I0123441

डायमंड

मानसशास्त्र शब्दकोश

इंग्रजी-मराठी-इंग्रजी

संकलन

प्रा. मुकुंद इनामदार

डायमंड पब्लिकेशन्स, पुणे

डायमंड मानसशास्त्र शब्दकोश इंग्रजी–मराठी–इंग्रजी

प्रा. मुकुंद इनामदार
१४, गणंजय सोसायटी, युनिट ४,
कोथरूड, पुणे ४११ 0३९ फोन : २५३८0९११

प्रथम आवृत्ती – ५ फेब्रुवारी २००९

ISBN 978-81-8483-083-5

© डायमंड पब्लिकेशन्स, पुणे – ३0

अक्षरजुळणी :
अक्षरवेल, पुणे

मुखपृष्ठ :
शाम भालेकर

प्रकाशक :
दत्तात्रेय गं. पाष्टे
डायमंड पब्लिकेशन्स,
१६९१, सदाशिव पेठ, शंकरप्रसाद को. हौ. सो.
तिसरा मजला, टिळक रोड, पुणे ४११०३०.
☎ ०२० – २४४५२३८७

प्रमुख वितरक :
डायमंड बुक डेपो
६६१, नारायण पेठ, अप्पा बळवंत चौक,
पुणे ३०. ☎ ०२० – २४४८०६७७

मूल्य रु. : १४०/-

प्रकाशकीय

डायमंड शब्दकोश मालिकेतील मानसशास्त्र विषयाचा शब्दकोश सादर करताना मला अत्यंत आनंद होत आहे. एखादी नवी कल्पना, नवा प्रयोग प्रत्यक्षात साकार झाला, की जे समाधान वाटते त्याचाच अनुभव मी आत्ता घेत आहे.

अर्थशास्त्र, मानसशास्त्र, राज्यशास्त्र, समाजशास्त्र, भूगोल, इतिहास अशा वेगवेगळ्या विषयांचा अभ्यास मराठीतून करताना विद्यार्थ्यांना अनेक समस्या येतात. कधी एखाद्या संज्ञेचे इंग्रजी नाव अधिक परिचयाचे असते, परंतु त्याचा अर्थ नेमका माहीत नसतो, तर कधी इंग्रजी शब्दांना दिलेल्या मराठी पारिभाषिक शब्दांचा अर्थ उलगडत नाही. या सर्व समस्यांचे निराकरण करू शकणारा शब्दकोश तयार करण्याचे बरेच दिवस मनात होते. आता इतर वेगवेगळ्या विषयावरील शब्दकोशही लवकरच सादर करण्याचा मानस आहे. प्रत्येक विषयावरील अनुभवी व तज्ज्ञ व्यक्तींची मोलाची मदत या कामी लाभली हे माझे भाग्यच !

हे काम जास्तीत जास्त अचूकतेने करण्याचा आम्ही प्रयत्न केला आहे. विद्यार्थी, अभ्यासक, प्राध्यापक यांचा उत्तम प्रतिसाद मिळेल ही आशा आहे.

दत्तात्रेय गं. पाष्टे

शब्दकोश सादर करताना....

महाविद्यालयातील मानसशास्त्राच्या अध्यापनापासून सेवानिवृत्तीपर्यंतच्या दीर्घ कालावधीत दोन गोष्टी प्रकर्षाने जाणवत राहिल्या, एक मानसशास्त्र विषयाचे विद्यार्थ्यांमध्ये कमालीचे आकर्षण वाढत चालले आहे आणि दोन, बहुसंख्येने या विषयाकडे वळलेल्या मराठी माध्यमाच्या विद्यार्थ्यांना सुबोध व सफाईदार मराठीतून व्याख्यान देणे ही महाविद्यालयीन शिक्षकांसाठी एक कसोटी पहाणारी कसरत आहे. याचे कारण काव्यभाषा किंवा ललितसाहित्याची भाषा म्हणून मराठी भाषेची क्षमता अमृताला जिंकण्याची असली, तरी विविध शास्त्रांची परिभाषा म्हणून तिचे सामर्थ्य पूर्णपणे प्रकट झालेले नाही – मानसशास्त्राच्या परिभाषेची मराठीतून अपेक्षित असलेली शब्दसंपत्तीची टांकसाळ कोठेही अस्तित्वात आलेली नाही. तशी गरज मात्र मराठीतून मानसशास्त्राचे अध्ययन / अध्यापन करणाऱ्यांना सातत्याने आणि तीव्रतेने जाणवत आहे.

इंग्रजी–मराठी मानसशास्त्रीय शब्दसंग्रहाच्या अभावी महाविद्यालयीन विद्यार्थ्यांचे व शिक्षकांचे पदोपदी चाचपडणे जवळजवळ दोन पिढ्या चालूच आहे. मानसशास्त्रीय संज्ञांचे आणि त्या अनुषंगाने विषयाचे नेमके आकलन होण्यासाठी आता इंग्रजी–मराठी शब्दकोशाची गरज आहे, हे डायमंड प्रकाशनाच्या श्री. द. गं. पाष्टे यांनी केवळ हेरलेच नाही, तर या गरजपूर्तीसाठी शब्दकोश प्रकाशित करण्याचे ठाम पाऊल उचलले, ही त्यांची उपक्रमशीलता दाद देण्यासारखी आहे.

या पार्श्वभूमीवर सादर होत असलेल्या सदर मानसशास्त्रीय शब्दार्थकोशात सुमारे पंधराशेहून अधिक संज्ञांचा व शब्दसमूहांचा समावेश झालेला असून त्यांची इंग्रजी मुळाक्षरक्रमानुसार मांडणी करण्यात आलेली आहे. प्रथम मूळ संज्ञा देऊन तिचा अर्थ इंग्रजीत शक्य तितक्या संक्षेपाने पण सुयोग्यपणे दिलेला असून शेवटी मराठी संज्ञा/शब्दसमूह देण्यात आलेले आहेत. मराठी परिभाषा रूढ होण्याच्या प्रक्रियेत असल्याने काही ठिकाणी पर्यायी संज्ञा/शब्दसमूह दिलेले आढळतील. याशिवाय मानसशास्त्रातील विकृतिवाचक संज्ञा, मानसशास्त्राच्या उपशाखा व महत्त्वाची इतर संबंधित शास्त्रे, नससंस्था व निगडित अशा संज्ञा तसेच मानसशास्त्रात वारंवार वापरल्या जाणाऱ्या संख्याशास्त्रीय संज्ञा, याच्यासाठी शेवटी चार परिशिष्टे समाविष्ट केलेली आहेत. याशिवाय संदर्भासाठी मानसशास्त्रातील संशोधक व विचारवंत यांची

यादी सोबत जोडलेली आहे. त्वरित संदर्भासाठी त्यांचा उपयोग होऊ शकेल.

मानसशास्त्र विषयाच्या जिज्ञासूंमध्ये मराठी माध्यमाचा अवलंब करणाऱ्या अभ्यासकांचा वर्ग पुष्कळच वाढलेला आहे. कनिष्ठ महाविद्यालयीन, पदवीपूर्व, पदवीचे तसेच पदव्युत्तर शिक्षण घेणारे विद्यार्थी, त्यांना शिकविणारा अध्यापकवर्ग, मराठीतून विषय–संशोधन करणारे साधक, स्पर्धा–परीक्षांमध्ये मातृभाषेतून परीक्षा देणारे स्पर्धक, आंतरशाखीय अभ्यास करणारे विद्याव्रती, इंग्रजीतील मानसशास्त्रीय साहित्याचा अनुवाद करू पहाणारे अनुवादक आणि अगदी दैनंदिन व्यवहारात मानसशास्त्रीय लिखाणाचे वाचन करणारे साधारण वाचक या सर्वांनाच हा शब्दार्थकोश उपयुक्त ठरेल अशी आशा आहे.

प्रस्तुत शब्दार्थकोश सर्वांगपरिपूर्ण आणि निर्दोष आहे, असा कोशरचनाकर्त्याचा दावा नाही. रूढ आणि विस्तृत परिभाषेचा अभाव, पर्यायी प्रतिशब्दाची उपलब्धता, चपखल अशा प्रतिशब्दांची कित्येक ठिकाणी जाणवणारी चणचण, संज्ञांची निवड व कोशव्याप्तीबाबत पडणाऱ्या व्यक्तिगत दृष्टिकोनाच्या मर्यादा या सर्व गोष्टींचा एक समुच्चयाने विचार करता एक अधिकारी मार्गदर्शक शब्दकोश असे म्हणण्याऐवजी शैक्षणिक व इतर दैनंदिन व्यवहारात साथ देणारा एक सहाय्यक शब्दकोश असा या प्रयत्नाचा उल्लेख सार्थ ठरावा. म्हणूनच विषयप्रभू व भाषाप्रभू व्यक्तींना असे नम्रतापूर्वक आवाहन करतो की त्यांनी आवश्यक त्या विधायक सूचना करून कोशाची कार्यक्षमता वर्धिष्णू करावी.

मानसशास्त्रीय इंग्रजी–मराठी शब्दार्थकोशाच्या अशा या जवळजवळ एकहाती प्रयत्नामागे, पूर्वसूरींच्या ऋणाचे केवळ कृतज्ञ स्मरण करणेच शक्य आहे. पेंग्विनचा बृहद् मानसशास्त्रीय इंग्रजी शब्दकोश, डेव्हिड स्टॅट, जॉन ग्रँड यांच्याबरोबरच अनमोलचा इंग्रजीतील शब्दकोश संदर्भ म्हणून मार्गदर्शक ठरले आहेत, डॉ. बी. आर. जोशी यांचा 'मराठी मानसशास्त्रीय संकल्पनाकोश' मराठी –शब्दरचनेच्या अंगाने उपयुक्त ठरला आहे. याखेरीज विषयवर्तुळातील काही अनुभवी मित्रांशी झालेली शब्दार्थचर्चा आणि मराठीतून उपलब्ध असलेली मानसशास्त्रावरील पाठ्यपुस्तके यांचा आधार कोशकामात उपयुक्त व निर्णायक ठरलेला आहे.

या सर्वांचे फलित शब्दचिकित्सक वाचक आणि मानसशास्त्राचे जिज्ञासू यांचेसमोर मांडले आहे. प्रतिसादाची सदैव प्रतीक्षा करत आहे.

प्रा. मु. कृ. इनामदार

डायमंड मानसशास्त्र - शब्दकोश

A

ability - (ॲबि'लिटी) **क्षमता** : a person's potential to do something.

ablation - (ॲबलेशन्) **(मेंदूच्या भागाची) छेदनशस्त्रक्रिया** : surgical removal of brain tissue.

abnormal behaviour - (ॲब्नॉ'र्मल् बिहे'व्ह्) **अपसामान्य वर्तन** : behaviour deviating from the normal accepted social rules.

abnormal psychology - (ॲब्नॉ'र्मल् साइकॉ'लजि) **अपसामान्य मानसशास्त्र** study of abnormal behaviour, its diagnosis and treatment in scientific way.

abreaction - (ॲ'ब्रेंबशन्) **तणावमुक्तीचा सुस्कारा सोडणे** : relief of tension experienced by patient in psychoanalysis.

absent - mindedness - (ॲ'ब्सेन्ट् माइन्डिड्नेस्) **भानावर नसणे** : not paying attention to those phases of situation which other's consider to be of major importance.

absolute threshold - (ॲ'ब्सल् (ल्यू)ट् थ्रे'श्होऽल्ड्) **निरपेक्ष सीमामूल्य** : the point at which a stimulus can just be picked up by the sense organs.

absolutism - (ॲब्सलू'टिझम्) **अंतिम / निर्विवाद-नियम** in moral judgment, children accept parents' verdict as ultimate i. e. absolutely true.

abstract intelligence - (ॲ'ब्स्ट्रॅक्ट् इन्टे'लिजन्स्) **अमूर्त बुद्धिमत्ता** : ability to use symbols and concepts to solve unfamiliar problems.

abstract learning - (ॲ'ब्स्ट्रॅक्ट् ल'र्निंग) **अमूर्त अध्ययन** : learning that does not involve concrete objects.

accident proneness - (ॲ'क्सिडन्ट् प्रोनेनस) **अपघात प्रवणता** : tendency of a person to have disproportionately large number of accidents.

accidental error - (ऑक्सिडे'न्टल् ए'रऽ) **आकस्मिक प्रमाद** : errors which arise in psychological experiments due to accidental factors.

accidental group - (ऑक्सिडे'न्टल् ग्रुप्) **आकस्मिक समूह** : the group whose members have come together accidently without a specific purpose.

accommodation - (अकॉमडे'ऽशन्) **संयोजन** : adjustment of a sense organ for a given stimulus .

achievement motive - (अची'व्हमन्ट् मो'ऽटिव्ह्) **संपादन-प्रेरक** : tendency to strive for success or attainment of a desired goal.

achievement test - (अची'व्हमन्ट् टेस्ट्) **कसोटी** : a standardised test that is designed to measure individual's level of knowledge in a specific area.

achromatic colors - (अक्रोमॅटिक कं'लऽ) **कृष्ण, श्वेत व राखाडी रंग** : black, white and grey colors.

achromatism - (ऑक्रोमॅटिझम) **पूर्ण रंगांधत्व** : total color blindness.

acoustic coding - (अक्'स्टिक् को'ऽडिन्) **ध्वनिस्वरूपातील संकेतन** : encoding words in terms of their sound using information in long term memory.

acquired characteristic - (ऍक्वा'अड् कं'रक्टरि'स्टिक्) **गुणवैशिष्ट्ये** : characteristic that is not innate / skill acquired by learning.

acquired drive - (अक्वा'अड् ड्राइव्ह्) **संपादित प्रेरणा** : the motivational force, arousal or satisfaction of which has been learned.

acquired status - (अक्वा'अड् स्टे'ऽटस्) **संपादित दर्जा** : a position that someone has achieved in society by efforts.

acquisition - (अं'क्विझि'शन) **संपादणूक/प्राप्ती** : learning and strengthening a response.

action potential - (अं'क्शन् पोऽटेन्शल) **क्रियाविभव** : the exchange of inside and outside ions of the neurons.

action slips - (अं'क्शन स्लिप) **नकळत घडलेली कृती** : actions that occur, not intended.

active sleep - (ऑक्टिव्ह् स्लीप) **सक्रीय निद्रा** : rem sleep.

actor-observer effect - (ॲ'क्टऽ अब्झ'ऽव्हऽ इफे'क्ट्) **कर्ता-निरीक्षक परिणाम :** the tendency of people to attribute their own behaviour to external causes but that of others to internal causes.

acute alcoholic hallucinations - (ॲक्यू'ट् अ'ल्कहॉलिक् हलू'सिने'ऽशन्) **तीव्र मद्यासक्ती संलग्न विभ्रमविकृती :** hallucinations caused by severe alcoholism.

adaptation - (ॲड'प्शन्) **प्रतियोजन :** structural or functional change for effective response to environment.

addiction - (ॲडि'क्शन्) **व्यसनासक्ती :** continuation of harmful and obsessive behaviour.

additive tasks - (ॲडि'टिव्ह् टाऽस्क्) **संयुक्त कामगिरी :** tasks carried out co-operatively and as a collective effort.

adjustment - (अजे'स्ट्मन्ट्) **समायोजन :** making suitable changes for effective relationship with the social setting.

adolescence - (ॲडले'सन्स्) **युवावस्था/किशोरावस्था :** the stage of life between childhood and adulthood.

adolescence growth spurt - (ॲडले'सन्स् ग्रोऽथ स्पऽट्) **किशोरवयीन जलद वाढीचा प्रस्फोट :** a period of rapid physical growth that accompanies the onset of puberty.

adrenal gland - ('ॲडरीनल् ग्लॅन्ड) **वृक्कस्थ ग्रंथी :** endocrine gland situated above kidneys involved in emotional experience.

adrenaline - (ॲडरीनलीन्) **वृक्कस्थ ग्रंथीस्राव :** hormone involved in expression of emotions.

adult psychology - (अडे'ल्ट् साइकॉ'लजि) **प्रौढांचे मानसशास्त्र :** refers to the psychological problems of persons beyond adolescence.

aetiology - (इटिऑलॉजि) **विकृतीमीमांसा :** the study of causes of a disease or disorder.

affect - (अफे'क्ट्) **भावानुभव :** experience of feelings & emotions.

affective disorder - (अफे'क्टिव्ह् डिसॉ'ऽडऽ) **भावनिक विक्षोभ विकृती :** emotional disorder.

afferent nerve - (ॲफरंट नर्व्ह) **वेदक नसतंतू :** the nerve sending messages from the sense organs to the brain.

affiliation - (अफि'लिए'ऽशन्) **सहवास/समूहभावना** : experiencing group membership.

after-image - (आ'ऽफ्टऽ इ'मिज्) **पश्चात् प्रतिमा** : continuation of a sensory experience after removal of the stimulus.

age - regression - (एऽज् रिग्रे'शन्) **वय-परागमन** : going back and experiencing the earlier stages of life during hypnotic trance.

ageing - (एऽजिन्ग्) **जराविज्ञान** : process of growing old and the study of old age.

aggression - (अग्रे'शन्) **आक्रमण** : a form of behaviour intended to injure others.

aggressiveness - (अॅग्रेसिव्हनेस) **आक्रमकता-प्रवृत्ती** : tendency to harm or intending to injure others.

agitation - (अॅजिटे'ऽशन्) **प्रक्षोभ** : state of restlessness.

agnosia - (अॅग्नॉ'सिआ) **प्रत्यभिज्ञाभाव/अर्थज्ञानाभाव/संवेदनाभाव** : failure of perception due to brain damage.

agoraphobia - (अॅ'गरफो'ऽबिअ) **खुल्या जागेचे भय** : fear of open places.

aha -experience - (अहा इक्स्पि'अरिअन्स्) **अहाहा (मर्मदृष्टीचा) अनुभव** : refers to the feeling that accompanies the moment of insight.

alcoholism - (अ'ल्कहॉलिझम्) **मद्यासक्ती** : state of addiction to alcohol.

Alexander's pass along test - (अलेक्झंडर्स पास-अॅलॉग टेस्ट) **अलेक्झांडर प्रारंभ-शेवट पार कसोटी** : performance test consisting of blocks for constructing desings according to the cards given.

alexia - (अलेक्शिया) **वाचन अक्षमता** : inability to read.

algorithms - (अल्गोरिदमस) **समस्यापरिहाराचे क्रमबद्ध नियम** : set of rules, specified in step by step order for solution of a problem

alienation - (ए'ऽल्यने'ऽशन) **परके होणे/तुटलेपण** : feelings or being estranged, separated and powerless in relation to oneself, society or nature.

all - or none principle - (ऑ'ऽल् ऑऽ नॅन् प्रि'न्सिपल्) **सर्व वा नैक-सिद्धान्त** : the principle which states that a neuron either responds completely or not at all.

Allport Vernon Lindzey-test - (ऑलपोर्ट व्हर्नन लिंडझे टेस्ट) **आल्पर्ट-व्हरनॉन-लिंडझे (मूल्यविषयक) कसोटी** : a test devised by the said three psychologist for person's preference for values.

alpha bias - (ॲ'ल्फ़s बा'इअस्) **लिंगभेद अतिगणन** : the tendency to exaggerate difference between sexes.

alpha rhythm - (ॲ'ल्फ़s रि'दम्) **अल्फा लहरी** : the type of brain waves formed in adults while resting.

Altered state of consciousness - (ऑल्टर्ड स्टेट् अव्ह कॉ'न्शसनिस्) **परिवर्तित बोधावस्था** : situations in which one's subjective experience is different from normal working consciousness.

alternative hypothesis - (ऑल्ट'sनटिव्ह हायपॉ'थिसिस्) **पर्यायी यथार्थ अभ्युपगम** : the experimental hypothesis, alternative to null hypothesis which claims that the findings in the study are not due to chance, but reflect true relationship.

altruism - (ॲ'लटुइझम्) **परहितवाद** : refers to unselfish act intended for the welfare for others.

Alzheimer's disease - (अल्झायमर्स डिसीज) **अल्झायमरची विकृती** : a degenerative brain disorder involving memory loss and disorientation.

ambivalence - (ॲम्बि'व्हलन्स्) **द्विधा मनःस्थिती** : tendency to oscillate between opposing mental states

ambivert - (ॲम्बि'व्हर्ट) **उभयमुखी (व्यक्तिमत्व)** : a person who is both extrovert and introvert.

amnesia - (ॲम्नी'झिअ) **स्मृतिलोप** : partial or complete loss of memory.

amygadalatomy - (ॲमिगडालाटॉमी) **ॲमिगडालाची शस्त्रक्रिया** destruction of amygadala involved in anger.

anaesthesia - (ॲ'निस्थी'झिअ) **भूल/संवेदनाभाव** : loss of sensitivity to stimulation which may be total or local.

anal expulsive personality - (ॲ'नल् इक्स्प'ल्सिव्ह प'sसनॅ'लिटि) **गुदोत्सर्जक व्यक्तिमत्व** : personality characterised by anal expulsiveness, i.e. passing of feces.

anal retentive personality - (ॲ'नल् रिटे'न्टिव्ह प'सनॅ'लिटि) **गुदावरोधक व्यक्तिमत्व** : personality characterised by anal retentiveness, i.e. with blocking of feces.

anal stage - (ॲ'नल् स्टेज्) **गुदावस्था** : second stage in infant's life, according to Freud when it is concerned with pleasure, received from anus.

analogies test - (अनॅ'लजिझ् टेस्ट) **सादृश्याधारित कसोटी** : mental test asking the subject to complete the fourth term, based on analogy.

analysand - (ॲनालीझन्ड) **मनोविश्लेषणाधीत व्यक्ती** : someone undergoing psychoanalysis

anecdotal - method - (ॲ'मिकडोऽटल् मे'थड्) **दंतकथा पद्धती** : method based on casual observation or heresay.

androcentric bias - (ॲन्ड्रोसेन्ट्रिक ब्रा'इअस) **पुरुषप्रधान दृष्टिकोन** : a bias in favour of males.

androgen - (ॲड्रोजेन) **पुरुष लैंगिक ग्रंथीस्त्राव** : male sex hormone.

animal psychology - (ॲ'निमल् साइकॉ'लजि) **प्राणिमानसशास्त्र** : branch of psychology dealing with systematic study of animal behaviour.

animism - (ॲ'निमिझम्) **वस्तुचैतन्यवाद** : the belief that inanmate things are animate living beings.

anorexia - nervosa - (ॲनॉरिक्सिया न'व्होसा) **चेतापदशा क्षुधाभाव** : disorder due to undereating.

anterograde amnesia - (ॲंटेरॉग्रेड ॲम्नी'झिअ) **उत्तरकालीन स्मृतीलोप:** loss of memory for experiences after the trauma.

anthropomorphism - (ॲ'न्थ्रपॉ'मॉ'ऽफिझम्) **मानुषीकरण** : tendency to see human qualities in non-humans.

anti - social behaviour - (ॲन्टिसो'ऽशल् बिहे'ऽव्हिअऽ) **समाजविरोधी वर्तन** : behaviour opposing accepted rules & customers of the society.

anxiety - (ॲन्झा'इअटि) **तणावग्रस्तता/चिंताग्रस्तता** : state of tension and worry.

anxiety neurosis - (ॲन्झा'इअटि न्यूरॉ'सिस्) **चिंताव्याकुल नसविकृती** : the neurotic condition caused by anxiety.

apathy - (ॲ'पथि) **वैफल्यजन्य उदासीनता** : indifference out of frustration.

aphagia - (ॲफेजिया) **अन्नग्रहण-अक्षमता/गिळण्याची अक्षमता** : inability to eat.

aphasia - (अफेशिया) **वाचाविकृती** : disorder of different aspects of language.

apnea - (ॲप्निया) **झोपेत श्वास कोंडण्याची विकृती** : sleep disturbance characterised by inhibited breathing during sleep.

apparent motion - (ॲपे'अरन्ट् मो'ऽशन्) **भासमान गती** : the illusion of movement created when similar stationery stimuli are presented in rapid succession.

apperception - (ॲपरसेप्शान) **अंतर्बोध/आसंवेदन** : the final stage in the process of perception where something is clearly understood.

applied psychology - (अप्ला'इड् साइकॉ'लजि) **उपयोजित मानसशास्त्र** : subdivisions within psychology that seek to apply principles of psychology to practical problems in different areas of behaviour.

appraisal - (अप्रेऽझल्) **(कार्य) मूल्यमापन** : an evaluation of how one has performed.

approach approach conflict - (ॲप्रो'ऽच्-अप्रो'ऽच् कॉ'न्फ्लिक्ट्) **प्रगमन- प्रगमन संघर्ष** : conflict caused by having to choose between two desirable objects or goals.

approach avoidance conflict - (ॲप्रो'ऽच् ॲव्हा'इडन्स् कॉ'न्फ्लिक्ट्) **प्रगमन वर्जन संघर्ष** : situation in which a person is confronted with an object or goal which is both attractive & unattractive at the same time .

aptitude - (ॲ'पृटिट्यूड्) **अभिक्षमता/अभियोग्यता** : the potential for acquiring a skill or ability after some training.

aptitude test - (ॲ'पृटिट्यूड् टेस्ट्) **अभियोग्यता चाचणी** : a test that tries to predict a person's capacity for acquiring a certain skill or ability.

archetype - (आऽच्टाइप्) **सामुदायिक अबोध मन** : the contents of collective unconscious, according to Jung.

arm chair method - (आऽम् चेअर मे'थड्) **आराम खुर्चीची पद्धत** : the method of contemplating over human behaviour without any objective observation, experiment or anyother scientific method.

army alpha test - (आ'ऽमि ॲ'ल्फऽ टेस्ट्) **आर्मी अल्फा कसोटी** : the first intelligence test used by U. S. army during world war I.

arousal level - (अरा'उझल् ले'व्हल्) **जागरण पातळी** : alertness of brain of a person to messages about external world via the senses.

articulatory phonological loop - (आऽटि'क्युलेऽट्री फोऽनॉ'लजिकल् लूप्) **उच्चारणशास्त्रीय बंध** : the 'inner voice' functioning as rehearsal system for one's own spoken words.

artificial code - (आ'ऽटिफि'शल् को'ऽड्) **मानवी कौशल्याधिष्ठित/कृत्रिम संकेत** : the non- verbal communication codes consisting of furniture, architecture, clothing etc. based on human skills.

artificial intelligence - (आ'ऽटिफि'शल् इन्टे'लिजन्स्) **कृत्रिम बुद्धिमत्ता** : the science of making machines (computer based) do things which are usually done by human intelligence.

assimilation - (असि'मिले'शन्) **संमीलन/समावेशन** : dealing with new situations by using existing congnitive organisation.

association - (असो'ऽशिएऽशन्) **साहचर्य** : a learned connection between two ideas or events.

association area - (असो'ऽशिएशन् ए'अरिअ) **सहयोजन/साहचर्य क्षेत्र** : areas of cerebral cortex that integrate inputs from various sensory channels.

asthenic - (एस्थेनिक) **कृशदेही** : having a very thin body.

ataxia - (अॅटेक्शिया) **कारक असूत्रता दोष** : partial or complete lack of muscle co-ordination.

athletic - (अॅथ्ले'टिक्) **स्नायुप्रधान/सुदृढ** : having strong muscular body.

attention - (अटे'न्शन्) **अवधान** : the focusing of perception leading to heightened awareness of stimuli.

attention divided - (अटे'न्शन् डिव्हा'इडेड) **विभाजित अवधान** : having to attend two or more inputs at the same time.

attention span - (अटे'न्शन् स्पॅन्) **अवधान कक्षा** : the length of time one is able to concentrate on a task at hand.

attention sustained - (अटे'न्शन् सस्टे'ऽन्ड्) **सातत्यपूर्ण अवधान** : continuous attention for a considerable long time.

attitude - (अॅ'टिट्यूड्) **अभिवृत्ती** : a like or dislike, a favorable or unfavorable evaluation of and reaction to an object, person or idea.

attitude scale - (अॅ'टिट्यूड् स्केऽल्) **अभिवृत्तीमापक श्रेणी** : a set of questions designed to elicit attitudes and measure their strength.

attribution - (अॅट्रिब्यु'शन्) **गुणरोपण प्रक्रिया** : assigning a certain characteristic.

audience - (ऑ'डिअन्स्) **श्रोतृवृंद** : a disciplined group of people which has a definite purpose for coming together such as for getting entertainment or knowledge.

authoritarian personality - (ऑथॉरिटे'अरिअन् प'ऽसर्नें'लिटि) **हुकुमशाही/ अधिकारशाही व्यक्तिमत्त्व** : an individual holding rigid beliefs, submissive to persons in authority but hostile towards weaker groups.

autism - (ऑटिझम) **स्वमग्नता** : the state of being lost in a world of inner fantasy.

auto suggestion - (ऑ'ऽटोऽ सजे'स्चन्) **स्वयंसूचना** : a suggestion coming from oneself with an object of attempting, consciously to produce change in one's behaviour.

autokinetic effect - (ऑ'ऽटोऽकायनेटिक इफे'क्ट्) **स्वयंजनितगतीचा परिणाम** : a visual illusion where a small spot of light in a darkened room appears to be moving when in fact it is stationary.

automatic priming - (ऑ'ऽटर्में'टिक् प्रा'इमिंग्) **स्वयंचलित प्रथमीकरण** : false consensus effect occurring even without knowledge of the stimulus.

autonomic nervous system - (ऑ'ऽटनॉ'मिक् न'व्हस् सि'स्टम्) **स्वायत्त- नससंस्था** : self regulating part of nervous system controlling vital function of the body.

autonomous morality - (ऑऽटॉ'नमस् मरॅ'लिटि) **हेतूकेंद्रीत नैतिक निर्णयः** morality where person's intentions are used as basis of judgement.

availability heuristic - (अव्हे'ऽलबि'लिटि ह्यअरि'स्टिक) **उपलब्धता नवगामी** : a mental shortcut based on how quickly instances come to mind.

aversion therapy - (अव्ह'ऽशन् थे'रपि) **तिटकारा उपचार पद्धती** : the form of treatment in which undesirable behaviour is eliminated by associating it with severe punishment.

avoidance avoidance-conflict - (अव्हॉ'इडन्स्-अव्हॉ'इडन्स कॉ'न्फ्लिक्ट्) **वर्जन-वर्जन संघर्ष** : conflict caused by having to choose between two undesirable objects or goals.

avoidance learning - (अव्हॉ'इडन्स् ल'र्निंग्) **परिहारात्मक अध्ययन** : learning to prevent an unpleasant situation by making a particular response to stimulus.

awareness - (अवे'अनेस) **जाणीव/बोधन** : consciousness of external or internal stimuli.

■

B

Babinski reflex - (बॅबिनस्की 'रीऽफ्लेक्स) **बॅबिन्स्की प्रतिक्षेप** : normal reflex occuring in infants below 2 years in which toes curl upwards when the sole of the foot is stroked.

babyhood - (बे'ऽबिहुड्) **शैशवावस्था** : early stage of childhood.

backward conditioning - (बॅ'क्वड कन्डि'शनिन्ग) **प्रतिगामी अभिसंधान** :classical conditioning where unconditioned stimulus is presented just before conditioned stimulus.

balance theory - (बॅ'लन्स् थि'अरी) **समतोलन सिद्धान्त** : tendency towards compatibility in beliefs because incompatibility causes tension.

bandwagon effect - ('बॅन्डवॅगन 'इफेक्ट) **लोकानुगामीप्रवृत्ती**: behavior of people attempting to conform to attitudes or actions of a group they identify with.

barbiturates - (बाऽ'बिच्युरेट्स्) **चिंताहारक शामके** : drugs widely used in the treatment of anxiety disorders.

Bard Cannon theory - (बाऽड 'कॅनन थि'अरी) **बार्ड-कॅनन-उपपत्ती** : a neurological theory of emotions stating that feelings from hypothalamus are experienced first and thereafter physiological activities come into existence.

basal age - (बेसल ए'ऽज) **आधारभूत वय** : indicates successfully clearing all items of mental tests.

basal metabolic rate (BMR) - (बेसल मिटॅ'बलिक रेऽट्) **आधार चयापचय प्रमाण** : the rate at which the body utilises energy at the state of rest.

basic mistrust- (बे'ऽसिक् ़मिस्ट्'स्ट्) **मूलभूत अविश्वास** : mistrust in oneself and the world caused by the pain of being thrust out of womb into external harsh world.

basic trust - (बे'ऽसिक् ट्रॅस्ट) **मूलभूत विश्वास** : trust created in the child because of love and care.

battle fatigue - (बॅ'ट्ल् फटी'ग) **युद्धजन्य थकवा / शीण** : psychological disorder resulting from exhaustion, stress and anxiety of warfare.

behavioural genetics - (बिहे'ऽव्हाऽल् जिने'टिक्स) **वर्तनात्मक जननीकशास्त्र:** the study of effects of genes on the expression of behaviour.

behaviour - (बिहे'ऽव्हाऽ) **वर्तन** : total collection of actions and reactions given by a person.

behaviour therapy - (बिहे'ऽव्हाऽ थे'रपि) **वर्तनोपचार पद्धती** : therapy designed to eliminate undesirable behaviour and to encourage desirable responses using behaviourist means.

behavioural therapy - (बिहे'ऽव्हाऽल् थे'रपि) **वर्तनवादी उपचारपद्धती** : clinical therapy based on learning principles associated with classical and operant conditioning.

behaviourism - (बिहे'ऽव्हरिझम्) **वर्तनवाद** : approach to psychology which rejects internal mental activity and focuses on obserable behaviour.

benzodiazepin - (बेन्झोडायझेपिन) **चिंताहारक औषधी द्रव्य** : anti anxiety drug.

Bernreuter personality inventory - (बर्नरुटर पर्सनॉलिटी इन्हेंटरी) **बर्नरूटर व्यक्तिमत्त्व कसोटी** : one of the earliest paper and pencil test of personality.

beta bias - (बी'टऽ बा'इअस) **लिंगभेद अवगणन** : the tendency to minimise sex differences.

beta rhythm - (बी'टऽ रि'दम्) **बीटा लहरी** : brain waves associated with mental activity.

biased sample - (बा'इअस्ड् सा'ऽम्पल्) **पूर्वग्रहदूषित नमुना** : the sample which is not representative of the population as a whole.

bilateral transfer - (बाइलॅ'टरल् ट्रॅ'न्स्फऽ) **द्विभागीय संक्रमण** : transferring a skill learned on one side of the body to the other side.

Binet scale - (बिनेऽ स्केऽल) **बिने श्रेणी** : test items invented by Alfred Binet for predicting child performance in school.

binocular cues - (बाइनॉ'क्युल क्यूऽज)) **द्विनेत्र नियामके** : visual cues about depth provided by information from both eyes.

binocular despairity - (बाइनॉ'क्युल (र) डि'स्पॅअरिटी)) **द्विनेत्र प्रतिमाभेद** : the image difference of any object on the two retinas.

binocular fusion - (बाइनॉ'क्युल फ्यू'झ्यन्) **द्विनेत्र प्रतिमा विलय** : fusion of two different images of an object from both eyes.

biofeedback method - (बा'इओ फीड् बॅक् मे'थड्) **जैव-प्रतिभरण पद्धती** : noting & considering physiological changes for treatment of the workers.

biological clock - (बाइऑ'लजिकल् क्लॉ'क) **जैविक घड्याळ** : a biological pacemaker that governs rhythms such as sleep-wake cycle.

biological psychology - (बाइऑ'लजिकल् साइकॉ'लजि) **जैव-मानसशास्त्र** : the branch of psychology dealing with the relationship between biological processes & behaviour.

birth order - (ब'ऽथ् ऑ'ऽडऽ) **जन्मक्रम** : the order of birth of children in a family.

birth trauma - (ब'ऽथ् 'ट्रॉऽमऽ) **जन्मकालीन (अवस्थांतराचा) धक्का** : shock of sudden transition from comfort of womb to harsh environment.

bisexuality - (बाइ'से'क्शुअॅलिटि) **उभयलिंगत्व** possessing the physical or psychological characteristics of both sexes.

blacky pictures - ('ब्लॅकी पि'क्चऽ) **श्वानव्यंगचित्र आधारित प्रक्षेपण तंत्र** : a projective technique for disturbed childern using cartoons about a family of dogs.

blind spot - (ब्लाइन्ड् स्पॉट्) **अंधबिंदू** : the area of retina, insensitive to light, where the optic nerve leaves the eye.

blindsight - (ब्लाइन्ड् साइट्) **अंधदृष्टी** : performing simple visual task despite no conscious awareness of seeing.

body language - (बॉ'डि ल'न्ग्विज्) **देहबोली** : non - verbal communication with other people by means of physical postures, gestures & body - movements.

boomerang effect - (बू'मरँग् इफे'क्ट) **प्रतिघात परिणाम** : attitude change in which someone changes his attitude in opposite direction from that being advocated.

border - line intelligence - (बॉ॒डउलाइन् इन्टे'लिजन्स्) **सीमागत बुद्धी** : an IQ score between 70 & 80 .

boredom (बॉ'डम्) **कंटाळा** : the psychological state produced by repetitive activity.

bottom - up process - (बॉ'टम्-अप प्रसे'स) **तल-ऊर्ध्व संस्करण** : gathering information directly from the external environment as distinct from the effects or expectations.

brain - waves - (ब्रेऽन् वेऽव्हज्) **मेंदू लहरी** : the recorded rhythms of the electrical activity of the brain.

brain localisation - (ब्रेंऽन् लो'कलाइझे'शन) **मेंदूतील स्थानिकीकरण** : the hypothesis that specific mental experiences or functions are associated with specific areas of brain.

brain potential - (ब्रेऽन प'टेन्शल) **मेंदूतील विद्युत क्रिया पातळी** : the level of electrical activity in the brain.

brain stimulation - (ब्रेऽन स्टि'म्युलेशन्) **मेंदू उत्तेजना** electrical stimulation of certain parts of brain for study of its function.

brain-stem - (ब्रेन स्टेम) **मेंदू स्कंध** : consisting of medula oblongata, part of brain pons, reticular formation and cerebellum.

brain storming - (ब्रेऽन स्टॉऽमिन्ग्) **मेंदू-वादळ** : free generation of ideas by members of a group for solving a specific problem.

brain washing - (ब्रेऽन वॉ'शिन्ग्) **मस्तिष्क प्रक्षालन** : physical, psychological or social pressure used for a radical change in behaviour.

break through - (ब्रेऽक्थ्रु) **समस्या भेद** : patient's sudden insight about a problem after overcoming resistance to dealing with it.

brightness constancy - (ब्राइट्नेस् 'कॉन्स्टन्सी) **तेजस्विता स्थिरता** : the experience of perceiving an object as maintaining the same level of brightness even though the objective illumination may change.

Broca's aphasia - (ब्रोकाज ॲफेशिया) **ब्रोकाची भाषा-अक्षमता** : speech disorder involving wrong and faltered pronunciations.

Broca's Area - (ब्रोकाज 'एअरीअ) **ब्रोकाचे वाचा क्षेत्र** : area of brain closely involved with producing speech.

bulimia nervosa - (बु'लिमीअ् न'व्होंसा) **क्षुधातिरेक-चेतापदशा** : an eating disorder in which excessive eating is followed by compensatory behaviour such as vomiting

bureaucratic leader - (ब्युअरॉऽक्रॅटिक ली'डऽ) **नोकरशहा** : the person who is appointed discharging leadership functions at same organisational level.

burnout - (बऽन्आउट्) **शीणवटा** : physical or emotional exhaustion produced especially by stress.

bystander apathy - (बा'इस्टॅ'न्डऽ अॅ'पथि) **प्रेक्षकाची निष्क्रिय अवस्था/ बघ्याची भूमिका** : tendency of people in a social situation not to go to the aid of strangers in an emergency.

■

California test of personality - (कॅलिफॉर्निआ टेस्ट अव्ह प'ऽसनॅ'लिटि) **व्यक्तिमत्त्वाची कॅलिफोर्निया कसोटी :** a widely used personality test based on the principle of life adjustment.

cannabis - (कॅनबीज) **कॅनबीज वनस्पती :** the plant from which marijuana drug is obtained.

cardinal trait - (का'ऽडिनल 'ट्रेऽट) **प्रधान-गुणघटक :** a pervasive and outstanding characteristic which influences nearly all of an individuals behaviour.

case history - (केऽस हि'स्टरि) **व्यक्तीवृत्त/ व्यक्तीइतिहास :** the biographical material obtained through interviews or collection of information from other sources like diaries etc.

castration anxiety - (कॅस्ट्रे'ऽशन ॲन्झा'इअटि) **खच्चीकरण चिंता :** childhood anxiety about being castrated as a punishment for harbouring sexual desire.

castration complex - (कॅ'स्ट्रेऽशन कॉ'म्प्लेक्स्) **लिंगछेदन गंड :** according to Freud, it is a complex caused in men by unconscious fears of losing penis, and in women by the fantasy of once having had a penis and then losing it.

catalepsy - ('कॅटलेप्सी) **स्नायुताठरता :** state of muscular rigidity associated with a hypnotic trance.

cataplexy - ('कॅटप्लेक्सी) **भीतीने थिजणे/ भयमूलक निश्चलता :** immobility caused by fear of shock.

catatonic - (कॅटअ्'टॉनिक) **काष्ठवत :** refers to a form of schizophrenia characterised by violent changes in behaviour.

catharsis - (कथा'र्सिस) **भावविरेचन** : purging of emotions by seeing them enacted on stage.

causal attribution - (कॉ'झल् ॲट्रिब्यु'शन्) **कारणिक गुणारोपण** : explaining behaviour by attributing causes.

cautious shift - (कॉशस् शिफ्ट) **समूह प्रभावित (सावध) निर्णय** : a form of group polarization where people make more cautious decisions under the influence of a group than by themselves.

central executive - (सेन्ट्रल एग्झे'क्युटिव्ह्) **केंद्रीय नियंत्रक** : the key component of working memory similar to 'paying' attention to something crucial in encoding process.

central fissure - (से'न्ट्रल् फि'शऽ) **मध्यवर्ती खाच** : fissure of each cerebral hemisphere that separates the frontal and parietal lobes, also known as fussure of Ralando.

central nervous system - (से'न्ट्रल न'व्हस् सि'स्टम्) **केंद्रीय नससंस्था** : part of nervous system that consists of brain & spinal cord.

central organizing trait - (सेन्ट्रल ऑ'ऽगनाइझिन्ग् ट्रेऽ) **केंद्रीय गुणघटक** : a trait that is characterstic of individual personality and associated with many other traits.

centration - (सेन्ट्रे'ऽशन) **एकांगी दृष्टी** : attending to only one aspect of situation.

cephalocaudal - (सीफॅलोकॉडल) **मस्तकापासून पायापर्यंत** : head tail.

cerebellum - (से'रिबेलम्) **लहान मेंदू** : part of brain, at the back and near the top of spinal cord.

cerebral cortex - (से'ख़िल् कॉऽटेक्स) **मेंदू पृष्ठ** : the surface layer of the forebrain or cerebrum made up of neurons.

cerebral hemispheres - (से'ख़िल् हे'मिस्फिर्स) **मेंदू गोलार्ध** : the two symmetrical left & right halves of cerebrum.

cerebrotonia - (सेरेब्रोटोनिआ) **विचारप्रधानता** : predominantly thinking characteristic of a personality.

character disorder - (कॅ'रक्टऽ डिसॉ'ऽडऽ) **चारित्र्य विकृती** : immaturity and general inability to cope with adult life.

charisma - (करि'झ्मऽ) **दैवी शक्ती** : the elusive quality of personality defined as 'personal magnetism' in relation to leadership.

chromosome - (क्रोमोसाम) **रंगसूत्रे** : thread like part of cell nucleus carrying genes.

child abuse - (चाइल्ड् अब्यू'स्) **बाल छळवणूक** : any treatment harming child's personality development.

child maltreatment - (चाइल्ड् मॅल्ट्री'टमन्ट्) **बाल-गैरवागणूक** : harmful behaviour towards child.

child psychology - (चाइल्ड् साइकॉ'लजि) **बालमानसशास्त्र** : branch of psychology dealing with child behaviour.

Choleric - (कॉ'लरिक) **चिडखोर** : irritable, touchy, easily angered

chronological age - (क्रॉ'नलॉ' जिक्ल् एऽज्) **जन्मवय** : age from the birth.

chunking - (चेन्किंग) **(माहितीचे) समूहीकरण/एकत्रीकरण** : process of combining items of information into longer meaningful units as an aid to memorising them.

cingulotomy - (सिन्युलोटॉमी) **सिंग्युलेट गायरसवरील शस्त्रक्रिया** : destruction of cingulate gyrus by electrical currents to reduce aggressive behaviour.

circadian rhythm - (सऽ'केइडीऽअन 'रिदम) **जैविक दिनचक्र** : a biological rhythm that recurs approximately every 24 hours.

circannual rhythm - (सऽक'ॲन्युअल 'रिदम) **जैविक वर्षचक्र** : a biological rhythm that recurs approximately once a year.

clair voyance - (क्ले'अव्हॉइअन्स्) **अतींद्रिय दृष्टी** : ability to see or perceive things without the use of eyes or sense organs.

classical conditioning - (क्लॅ'सिकल कन्डि'शनिन्ग्) **अभिजात अभिसंधान:** a basic form of learning in which simple responses are associated with new stimuli.

client centered therapy - (क्ला'इअन्ट् सेन्ट'ऽ थे'रपि) **रुग्ण-केंद्री उपचारपद्धती** : the humanistic therapy designed to increase the client's selfesteem.

clinical method - (क्लि'निकल मे'थड्)) **चिकित्सा पद्धती** : a kind of interview used by clinical psychologist for assessing mentally ill patients.

clinical psychology - (क्लि'निकल साइकॉ'लजि) **चिकित्सा-मानसशास्त्र** : branch of psychology dealing with emotional, mental or behavioural disorders and applying psychological research to their diagnosis & treatment.

clone - (क्लॉन) **फुटवा :** a sexual or artificial reproduction of living being.

closed group - (क्लउझड् ग्रूप) **बंदिस्त समूह :** a group whose membership is not readily available to any body.

closure - (क्लो'ऽझ्यऽ) **संपूर्णता तत्त्व :** built - in tendency of the brain to perceive incomplete things as complete.

co-acting group - (को'ॲक्टिन्ग ग्रूऽप) **सह-कार्यान्वित समूह :** a group whose members work independently for the same goal.

cocktail party effect - (कॉ'कऽटेऽल् पा'ऽटि इफे'क्ट) **मेजवानी परिणाम :** the ability to be aware of the physical characteristic of a non-attented message when focused on another conversation and tuning out all other noise.

cognition - (कॉ'ग्निशन्) **बोधानुभव :** all the mental processes by which one becomes aware of and gains knowledge about the world.

cognitive arousal theory - (कॉ'ग्निटिव्ह् अरा'उझल् थि'अरी) **बोधनिक जागरण उपपत्ती.**

cognitive behavioral therapy - (कॉ'ग्निटिव्ह् बि'व्हेरल् थे'रपि) **बोधात्मक वर्तनवादी उपचार पद्धती :** a development of congnitive therapy where some elements of behavioural therapy have been added.

cognitive bias - (कॉ'ग्निटिव्ह् बा'इअस्) **बोधात्मक पूर्वग्रह :** a predisposition to think in a certain way.

cognitive development - (कॉ'ग्निटिव्ह् डिव्हे'लपमन्ट्) **बोधात्मक विकास :** development of mental processes such as thought, reasoning and memory.

cognitive dissonance - (कॉ'ग्निटिव्ह् डि'सनन्स्) **बोधात्मक विसंवाद :** an unpleasant state of tension caused by two psychologically inconsistent cognitions or clash or one's behaviour with cognitions.

cognitive learning theory - (कॉ'ग्निटिव्ह् लऽनिंग् थि'अरी) **बोधात्मक अध्ययन उपपत्ती :** the theory, opposed to behaviourism, states that complex learning involves restructuring and reorganising of knowledge by the brain.

cognitive map - (कॉ'ग्निटिव्ह् मॅप) **बोधात्मक नकाशा :** a mental representation of spatial relationships in one's immediate environment.

cognitive mediational theory - (कॉ'ग्निटिव्ह् मे'डिटे'उशनल थि'अरी) **बोधात्मक मध्यस्थीविषयक उपपत्ती**

cognitive neuropsychology - (कॉ'ग्निटिव्ह् न्यूरॉ'साइकॉ'लजि) **बोधात्मक नसमानसशास्त्र** : study of workings of cognitive system through brain impairment associated with brain damage.

cognitive neuroscience - (कॉ'ग्निटिव्ह् न्यूरॉ'सा'इअन्स्) **बोधात्मक नसविज्ञान:** using various techniques for study of brain functioning to understand human cognition.

cognitive overload - (कॉ'ग्निटिव्ह् ओ'उव्हलॉउड्) **बोधात्मक अधिभार:** Receiving more information than one can process.

cognitive priming - (कॉ'ग्निटिव्ह् प्रा'इमिंग्) **आक्रमकताजनक बोधात्मक सूचना** : cues such as violent TV programmes leading to thoughts and feelings that produce aggression.

cognitive psychology - (कॉ'ग्निटिव्ह् साइकॉ'लजि) **बोधात्मक मानसशास्त्र** branch of psychology dealing with cognition, particularly the process of perception, learning language, memory and thinking.

cognitive restructuring - (कॉ'ग्निटिव्ह् रिस्ट्रि'क्चउरिंग) **बोधात्मक पुनर्रचना:** the technique used by cognitive therapists to make distorted beliefs more rational.

cognitive therapy - (कॉ'ग्निटिव्ह् थे'रपि) **बोधात्मक उपचार पद्धती** : the treatment dealing with person's emotional distortions and attempting to change or restructure his cognitions.

cognitive triad - (कॉ'ग्निटिव्ह् ट्रा'इअॅड्) **बोधात्मक त्रयी** : negative thoughts about the self, world and future found in depressed clients.

cohesiveness - (कोउही'सिव्हनेस्) **संसक्ती, संलग्नता** : attachment among members of a group and their unity.

cold emotion - (कोउल्ड् इमो'उशन्) **कृत्रिम भावना** : a psychological state resulting from injection of adrenaline.

collective leadership - (कले'क्टिव्ह् ली'डउशिप्) **सामूहिक नेतृत्व** : the form of leadership where power of decision and administration is allotted to a group rather than a single person.

collective mind - (कले'क्टिव्ह् माउइन्ड) **समूह मन** : the idea that there is a group mind over and above minds of individual composing the group.

colour blindness - (कॅ'लऽ 'ब्लाऽइन्डनेस) **रंगांधत्व** : partial or total inability to distinguish colours.

colour constancy - (कॅ'लऽ कॉ'न्स्टन्सि) **रंगसातत्य** : the tendency for an object to be perceived as having the same colour under varying viewing conditions.

colour contrast - (कॅ'लऽ कन्ट्रा'ऽस्ट्) **रंग विरोध** : the tendency for the difference between two colours to be intensified when placed side by side.

colour vision - (कॅ'लऽ व्हि'इ्यन्) **रंगदृष्टी** : the process by which the eye discriminates between different wave - lengths, providing the experience of different colours.

combat motive - (कॅ'म्बट/कॉ'म्बॅट् मो'ऽटिव्ह) **युयुत्सा प्रेरक** : the motive which enables a person to remove the obstacles in the way of goal fulfillment and to fight for winning over the situation.

common knowledge effect - (कॉऽमन् नॉ'लिज् इफे'क्ट्) **सर्वसामान्य ज्ञानाचा परिणाम** : the decision made by general agreement is not affected by a few members holding different opinions and thoughts.

common sense knowledge - (कॉऽमन् सेन्स नॉ'लिज्) **सामान्य पातळीवरील ज्ञान** : popular beliefs current in common experience not backed by scientific reasoning.

communication - (कम्यू'निके'ऽशन्) **संप्रेषण** : the process by which message sent by the sender is received by the receiver.

communicator credibility - (कम्यू'निकेटऽ क्रे'डिबिलिटि) **संप्रेषकाची विश्वासार्हता:** extent to which the communicator of a message is believable.

community - (कम्यू'निटि) **जमात** : a group of people living together with some specific goal and residing in a definite geographical area.

community psychology - (कम्यू'निटि साइकॉ'लजि) **जमातीचे मानसशास्त्र** : the branch of psychology combining clinical & social psychological principles to promote well being of psychologically disturbed people.

comparative psychology - (कम्पॅ'रटिव्ह साइकॉ'लजि) **तुलनात्मक मानसशास्त्र** : branch of psychology studying similarities & differences in the mental processes & behaviour of different species.

compensation - (कॉम्पिन्से'ऽशन्) **प्रतिपूरण :** defence mechanism in which a person seeks to make up for the short - comings by substituting some other characteristic.

competition - (कॉ'म्पिटि'शन) **स्पर्धा :** two or more individuals or groups seeking the same goal independently, are said to be in competition.

completion Test - (कम्प्ली'शन टेस्ट) **पूर्तता चाचणी :** a psychological test that requires the subject to fill in the missing letter, word or phrase.

complex - (कॉ'म्प्लेक्स्) **गंड :** a group of repressed, emotionally charged ideas that conflict with other ideas that the individual is conscious of

compliance - (कम्प्ला'इअन्स्) **अनुपालन :** confirming to the majority in order to be liked, or to avoid ridicule.

compromise - (कॉ'म्प्रमाइझ) **तडजोड :** a two way interaction between individuals or groups that abandon some part of their original claims or demands for better accommodation.

compulsion - (कम्पे'ल्शन) **अनिवार्य कृती, अनिवार्यता :** a repetitive action that a person feels driven to make and is unable to resist.

conation - (क'नेऽशन) **संकल्प :** a psychological activity which is described as impulse, desire, will and striving.

concept formation - (कॉ'न्सेप्ट फॉऽ'मेऽशन) **संकल्पना घडण :** abstracting the essential qualities of individual things and classifying them by higher order rules.

concrete intelligence - (कॉ'न्क्रीट् इन'टेलिजन्स) **मूर्त बुद्धिमत्ता :** ability to function effectively with concrete problems.

concrete operation stage - (कॉ'न्क्रीट् ऑपरे'ऽशन स्टेज्) **मूर्त क्रियात्मक अवस्था :** ability to deal with problem presented in concrete way according to Piaget.

concrete thinking - (कॉ'न्क्रीट् थिं'किंग) **मूर्त विचार :** thinking in concrete rather than in abstract terms.

concrete thinking - ('कॉन्क्रीऽट थिन्किंग) **मूर्त-विचारप्रक्रिया :** thinking that is rigidly confined to experiences of the concrete object.

conditioned response - (कन्डि'शन्ड् रिस्पॉ'न्स्) **अभिसंधित प्रतिक्रिया :** the response resulting solely from the process of conditioning

conditioned stimulus (कन्डि'शन्ड् स्टि'म्युलस्) **अभिसंधित उद्दिपक** : the stimulus originally ineffective in producing a given response but becomes effective after the process of conditioning.

conditioning - (कन्डि'शनिन्ग्) **अभिसंधान प्रक्रिया** : a process of learning where a given stimulus produces a response other than its normal, natural or automatic one.

cones - (कोऽन्स्) **शंकूपेशी** : photoreceptors in the retina of the eye that are specialised for colour - vision and sharpness of vision.

confabulation - (कॉन्फॅ'ब्युलेऽशन्) **असत्य कथनाची स्मृतीतील सरमिसळ:** filling blanks in the memory with plausible stories that are untrue but not deliberate lies.

confirmation bias (कॉ'न्फमे'ऽशन् बा'इअस्) **अनुकूलता-पूर्वग्रह/पुष्टि पूर्वग्रह:** a preference for evidence that supports rather than disapproves our predictions.

conflict - (कॉ'न्फ्लिक्ट्) **संघर्ष** : simultaneous presence of opposing or mutually exclusive inpulses, desires or tendencies.

conformity influence - (कन्फॉ'ऽमिटि इन्फ्लुअन्स्) **अनुसरिता-प्रभाव** : adopting the behaviour, attitudes or values of the majority after being exposed to their values or behaviour.

confounding variables - (कन्फा'उन्डिग् व्हे'रिएबल्स्) **सहवर्ती परिवर्तक:** variables mistakenly manipulated or allowed to vary along with independent variable.

congenital : (कन्जे'निटल्) **जन्मोद्भव** : something present at birth but not necessarily genetically inherited or innate .

connectionism - (कने'क्शनिझम्) **समांतर वितरित माहिती संस्करण** : the parallel distributed processing theory.

conscience - (कॉ'न्शन्स्) **सदसद्विवेक** : an internal recognition of standards of right and wrong by which individual judges his or her conduct.

consciousness - (कॉ'न्शस्निस्) **बोधावस्था** : the awareness of oneself in every aspect of one's being.

consolidation - (कन्सॉ'लिडे'ऽशन्) **दृढीकरण, एकत्रीकरण :** physiological changes that take place in the brain which help fix learned item in the memory.

constant error - (कॉ'न्स्टन्ट् ए'रऽ) **स्थिर प्रमाद :** error that occurs in psychophysical experiments due to either underestimation or overestimation about measurements.

consumer psychology - (कन्स्यू'मऽ सायकॉ'लजि) **ग्राहक मानसशास्त्र :** the study of behaviour of people as buyers and consumers of goods and services.

contact hypothesis - (कॉ'न्टॅक्ट् हाइपॉ'थिसिस्) **संपर्क अभ्युपगमः** the idea that mere contact between groups can reduce prejudice.

context dependent learning - (कॉन्टे'क्स्ट् डिपे'न्डन्ट ल'ऽनिंग्) **संदर्भसापेक्ष अध्ययन :** recall is better when it occurs in the same context as original learning.

contiguity - (कॉ'न्टिग्यु'इटि) **समीपता (तत्त्व) :** tendency to associate stimuli that occur close together in time & space.

continuity - (कॉ'न्टिन्यू'इटि) **सातत्य (तत्त्व) :** tendency to perceive stimuli as belonging with each other and forming a pattern if they follow each other closely and regularly in time & space.

continuous reinforcement - (कन्टि'न्युअस् रीइन्फॉ'ऽस्मन्ट्) **निरंतर/अखंड प्रबलन :** schedule of operant conditioning where reinforcement is given after every response.

contra suggestion - (कॉ'न्ट्रसजेस्चन्) **प्रति-सूचना :** acting in completely opposite way of a given suggestion.

contralateral - (कॉ'न्ट्रलॅ'ट्रल्) **विरुद्ध बाजूचे :** function on one side of the body are controlled by opposite cerebral hemisphere.

control group - (कन्ट्रो'ऽल् ग्रूप) **नियंत्रक गट :** a group of subjects sharing the same conditions as experimental group except exposure to experimental variable.

conventional stage - (कन्व्हे'न्शनल् स्टेज्) **परंपरानुसारी अवस्था :** a stage of moral development where people judge moral actions in terms of what other people think.

convergent thinking - (कन्व्हजन्ट थिं'किंग्) **एकदिश विचार** : thinking along conventional lines to find best single answer to a problem.

conversion hysteria - (कन्व्हं'ऽशन् हिस्टि'रिअ) **रूपांतरणात्मक उन्माद** : psychological disorder transformed into physiological symptoms.

co-operation - (को'ऽऑपरे'ऽशन्) **सहकार्य** : a two way interaction in which a common goal is achieved by mutual assistance.

coping strategies - (को'ऽपिंग् स्ट्रॅ'टिजिस्) **परिस्थितीशी सामना करण्याच्या युत्त्याः** skills developed through experience of life situations.

corpus collosam - (कॉ'ऽपस् कलोसम्) **महासंयोजी पिंड** : the connecting portion between two hemispheres of the brain.

correlation - (कॉ'रिले'ऽशन्) **सहसंबंध** : an association found between two variables.

correlation coefficient - (कॉ'रिले'ऽशन् कॉ'इफि'शन्ट्) **सहसंबंध-सहगुणकः** : the ratio that measures the extent to which variables are related.

correlational studies - (कॉ'रिले'ऽशनल् स्टडिज्) **सहसंबंधात्मक अभ्यास** : research designed to examine the nature of relationship between two or more naturally occurring variables.

cortex - (कॉऽटेक्स्) **(मेंदू) बाह्यक** : the outermopst surface of the the cerebrum.

co-twin control - (कॉ'व्टिन कन्ट्रो'ऽल्) **जुळ्या प्रयुक्तांवरील निमंत्रण** : an experiment in which one of the twins is subjected to independent variable while the other is not.

counselling psychologist - (का'उन्सलिंग सायकॉ'लजिस्ट्) **सल्ला मानसशास्त्रज्ञ** a trained & qualified psychologist working in non medical setting and dealing with personal problems such as academic, social or vacational not classified as illness.

counterconditioning - (का'उन्टऽ कन्डि'शनिन्ग्) **प्रति अभिसंधान** : substituting a relaxation response for a fear response to threatening stimuli in systematic desensitisation.

counterculture - (का'उन्टऽ कं'ल्चऽ) **प्रति संस्कृती** : way of life opposed to dominant culture in the society.

counter transference - (का'उन्ट्ऽ ट्रॅ'न्स्फरन्स्) **प्रति भावान्तरण** : psy-choanalysist's transference on to his patients.

courtesy bias - (क'ऽटिसि बा'इअस्) **सौजन्य-पूर्वग्रह** : responding without harming another's feelings.

covert - (कॅ'व्हट्ऽ) **अप्रकट/अव्यक्त** : process that cannot be directly observed.

creative thinking - (क्रिए'ऽटिव्ह् 'थिन्किन्ग) **सर्जनशील विचार** : thinking going beyond conventional thought process and bringing novel solutions to problems.

criminal psychology - (क्रि'मिनल सायकॉ'लजि) **अपराध मानसशास्त्र** : branch of psychology that deals with the study of criminal behaviour.

criterion group - (क्राइटि'अरिअन् ग्रूप) **निकष समूह** : a group of people of known characteristics, achievement or behaviour who are used as a standard for comparison.

cross cultural psychology - (क्रॉस् कॅ'ल्चरल् सायकॉ'लजि) **आंतर-सांस्कृतिक मानसशास्त्र** : an approach in which different cultures are studied and compared.

crowding behaviour - (क्राउडिन्ग् बिहे'ऽव्हऽ) **झुंडीतील वर्तन** : supposed response of animals or humans to the effects of being crowded.

crystallized intelligence - (क्रि'स्टलाइइड् इन्टे'लिजन्स्) **स्फटिकरूप बुद्धिमत्ता:** intelligence based on experience and skills acquired.

cue- dependent forgetting - (क्यू डिपे'न्डन्ट् फगे'टिन्ग) **सूचकाभावी घडणारे विस्मरण / सूचकाधारित विस्मरण** : forgetting due to absence of suitable cue.

cultural lag - (कॅ'ल्चरल् लॅग) **सांस्कृतिक गतिमांद्य** : continued use of old & ineffective ways of doing things even after introduction of effective means for achieving goals of a society.

cultural relativism - (कॅ'ल्चरल् रे'लटि'व्हिझम) **सांस्कृतिक सापेक्षतावाद :** the view that proper judgement of human behaviour is possible only with reference to the context of different cultures.

culture fair test - (कॅ'ल्चरल् फेअ'टेस्ट) **संस्कृती निर्दोष चाचणी** : test which claims removal of drawbacks of cultural setting.

culture free test - (कॅ'ल्चऽ फ्री टेस्ट) **संस्कृती मुक्त चाचण्या** : psychological tests from which influences or advantages of particular cultural experiences are eliminated.

curiosity - (क्यु'अरिऑं'सिटि) **जिज्ञासा** : the motive which is related to getting familiar to unfamiliar things.

curve of forgetting - (कऽव्ह् अव्ह् फगे'टिन्ग्) **विस्मरण वक्र** : the graphic representation of rate at which forgetting occurs.

cybernetics - (सायब'ऽनेटिक्स्) **मस्तिष्क संवहनशास्त्र** : science concerned with regulatory mechanisms and associated communication systems involving information feed back, found in brain functioning as well.

■

D

Darwinian reflex - (डार्विनिअन् री'फ्लेक्स्) **डार्विन प्रतिक्षेप/पकड-प्रतिक्षेप :** a grasping reflex found in human infants.

day - care - (डेऽ केअ) **शिशु संगोपन सेवा :** temporary care provided by people other than relatives to infant.

day dream - (डेऽ ड्रीम्) **दिवास्वप्न :** experiencing fantacies while one is awake.

death instinct - (डेथ् इ'न्स्टिक्ट्) **मरणप्रवृत्ती, संहारप्रवृत्ती :** instinct for destruction and death.

debriefing - (डि'ब्री'फिन्ग्) **प्रयोगपश्चात निवेदन :** telling the subject about the details including deception if any, after the experiement is carried out.

decentration - (डी'सेन्ट्रेऽशन) **सर्वांगीण विचार / सर्वस्पर्शी विचार :** the ability to focus on more than one aspect of a problem, according to Piaget.

deception - (डिसे'प्शन) **वंचना-तंत्र/दिशाभूलतंत्र :** a research technique providing false information to persons participating in a study.

decision making - (डिसि'झ्यन् मे'ऽकिंग) **निर्णयाप्रत येणे :** a preparatory stage for taking action where a person comes to certain conclusion after reflective thinking.

declarative knowledge- (डे'क्लरे'ऽटिव्ह नॉ'लिज) **वस्तुस्थितीजन्य ज्ञान :** factual knowledge

declarative memory - (डे'क्लरे'ऽटिव्ह मे'मरि) **(वस्तुस्थिती) वाचक स्मृती, निर्देशात्मक स्मृती :** memory related to factual information.

decoding - (डी'को'ऽडिन्) **विसंकेतन** : translating signals into messages.

deductive reasoning - (डिड'क्टिव्ह री'झनिन्) **विगमनात्मक विचार** : reasoning in which conclusions are not false if premises are ture.

deep processing - (डीप् प्र'सेसिन्) **तपशीलवार/सखोल संस्करण** : encoding for meaningful information.

deep relaxation - (डीप् री'लॅक्से'ऽशन) **पूर्ण शिथिलता** : breathing technique for complete relaxation & release of tension.

defence mechanism - (डिफे'न्स मे'कनिझम्) **हेतू संरक्षक यंत्रणा** : behaviour patterns which protect the ego from anxiety, shame or guilt.

defensive attribution - (डिफे'न्सिव्ह ऑट्रिब्यु'शन्) **बचावात्मक गुणारोपण:** blaming the victim of misfortune as a way of avoiding the anxiety provoking thoughts thus defending oneself.

deindividuation - (डि'इ'न्डिव्हि'ड्युएऽशन) **व्यक्तिमत्त्व विलय** : loss of sense of individual identity as found in crowd behaviour.

Delayed reaction - (डिले'ऽ री'ऑक्शन) **विलंबित प्रतिक्रिया** : refers to response in a reaction time experiment which does not occur immediately.

delayed reciprocal altruism - (डिले'ऽ रिसि'प्रक्ल् अँ'लट्रुइझम्) **विलंबित प्रतिपरोपकार अपेक्षा** : the altruistic act which is expected to be returned at a later stage.

delinquency - (डिलि'न्क्वन्सि) **गुन्हेगारी/अपराध वर्तन** : committing a crime or violating the legal code.

delirium - (डिलि'रिअम्) **भ्रांती** : an altered state of consciousness charcterised by delusions, hallucinations & illusions.

delusion of grandeur - (डिल्यू'झ्यन् अव्ह गॉ'न्ड्युअ) **थोरत्त्व विभ्रम** : the delusion that one is celebrated or exalted.

delta waves - ('डेल्टअ् 'वेऽव्हज्) **डेल्टा लहरी** : large and slow brain waves occurring only in deep sleep.

delusion - (डिल्यू'झ्यन्) **मतिभ्रम/विभ्रम** : false belief not supported by reason.

delusion of persecution - (डिल्यू'झ्यन् अव्ह प'ऽसिक्यूश'न्) **छळ विभ्रम:** the delusion of individual that his problems are caused by other people conspiring against him.

dementia - (डिमे'न्शिआ) **अवमनस्कता** : mental deterioration due to organic cause.

democratic leader - (डे'मक्रॅ'टिक् ली'डऽ) **लोकशाहीवादी नेता** : the leader that takes decisions with his followers and in the interest of group and acts accordingly.

dendrite - ('डेनड्राइट) **शिखातंतू** : the receiving end of the neuron.

denial - (डिना'इअल्) **नकार, अस्वीकार** : a defence mechanism that simply denies thoughts, feelings or wishes which cause anxiety.

dependence (डिपे'न्डन्स्) **अवलंबन** : having a need for the person or a thing to go about one's regular activities.

dependent variable - (डिपे'न्डन्ट् व्हे'अरिअब्ल्) **परतंत्र (अवलंबी) परिवर्तक:** the variable whose measured changes are attributed to changes in the independent variable.

depenetration - (डीपे'निट्रेऽशन्) **अंतरंगप्रवेश निषेध स्ववृत्तकथनसंकोच** : deliberately reducing the amount of self-disclosure to someone else.

depressant - (डि'प्रेसन्ट) **शामक** : a psychoactive drug that tends to reduce arousal.

depression - (डिप्रे'शन्) **खिन्नता/अवसादावस्था** : a mood disorder characterised by sadness and dejection.

deprivation - (डे'प्रिव्हे'ऽशन्) **वंचितता** : loss or removal of something which is desired.

depth interview - (डे'प्थ् इ'न्ट'व्ह्यू) **सखोल मुलाखत** : interview designed to get at underlying motivational factors behind observed behaviour.

depth perception - (डे'प्थ् पसे'पशन) **अंतराचे खोलीचे संवेदन** : perception of the depth viewing the world in three dimensions.

depth psychology - (डे'प्थ साइकॉ'लजि) **मनोगहन मानसशास्त्र** : the branch of psychology which seeks to explain the behaviour at the level of unconscious.

descriptive method - (डिस्क्रि'प्टिव्ह् मे'थड्) **वर्णनात्मक पद्धती** : the method which gives factual statement of the behaviour of animals or humans.

descriptive statistics - (डिस्क्रि'प्टिव्ह् स्टटि'स्टिक्स्) **वर्णनात्मक संख्याशास्त्र:** statistics that summarises a set of measurements.

desensitisation - (डीसे'न्सिटाइझ्झेशन्) **अवेदनशीलन** : decreased emotional sensitivity with respect to personal or social problems after counselling.

distractor - (डिस्ट्रॅ'क्टर) **अवधान विचलक** : the factor obstructing attention process.

deterrent theory of punishment - (डिटे'रन्ट् थि'अरी अव्ह प'निश्मन्ट) **शिक्षेची निवारणवादी उपपत्ती** : punishment intended for preventing criminal behaviour.

developmental intervention - (डिव्हे'लप्मन्टल इ'न्टव्हे'न्शन) **विकासात्मक आंतरनिरसन** : any proceduire or technique that is designed to interrupt, interfere with and modify an ongoing process for development purpose.

developmental method - (डिव्हे'लप्मेन्ट्ल् मे'थड्) **वैकासिक पद्धती** : method applied in psychological research which unfolds development stages in behaviour.

developmental psychology - (डिव्हे'लपमेन्ट्ल् साइकॉ'लजि) **वैकासिक मानसशास्त्र** : branch of psychology dealing with pre & post natal growth and maturation or behaviour.

developmental tasks - (डिव्हे'लप्मेन्ट्ल् टाऽस्क) **वैकासिक कार्ये** : skills achieved at certain ages for the successful adjustment by the individual.

deviation - (डी'व्हिए'शन्) **विचलन** : departure from the norm

dexterity test - (डेक्स्टे'रिटि टेस्ट्) **हस्तनैपुण्य कसोटी** : tests measuring speed and accuracy in manual operations.

diabolism - (डा'इअबॉ'लिझम) **सैतानीकरण** : attributing to a person or group attributes of the devil.

diagnostic & statistical manual (DSM) - (डा'इअग्नॉस्टिक अॅन्ड् स्टटि'स्टिकल् मॅं'न्युअल) **निदानात्मक आणि संख्याशास्त्रीय हस्तपुस्तिका** : a multiaxial system used for classifying & diagnosing over 200 disorders published by APA.

diagnostic test - (डा'इअग्नॉस्टिक् टेस्ट्) **निदानात्मक कसोटी** : test used by psychologist for probing of a mental or emotional difficulty.

diagonally opposite transfer - (डाइॲ'गऩलि ऑ'पझ़िट् टॅन्स्फ's) **विरुद्ध पक्षीय संक्रमण** : transfer of learning from one side of the body to diagonally opposite side of the body.

difference threshold - (डि'फ्रन्स थ्रे'श़्हो'ल्ड्) **भेदनिक सीमामूल्य** : the minimum difference between a pair of stimuli that can be perceived under experimental condition.

differential aptitude test - (डि'फरेन्शल् ॲ'प्टिट्यूड टेस्ट्) **विविध भिन्नतादर्शक अभिक्षमता कसोटी** : aptitude test designed for selection in industrial field.

differentiation - (डि'फरे'न्शिएऽशन्) **भेदनीकरण** : making different responses to similar looking stimuli.

diffusion of responsibility - (डिफ्यू'झ्यन् अव्ह रिस्पॉ'न्सिबि'लिटि) **जबाबदारीचे विकिरण** : bearing a small portion of responsibility.

digit span test - (डि'जिट स्पॅऽन टेस्ट) **अंकविस्तार कसोटी** : experiment for determining digits a person is able to recall immediately after presenting them.

Dilemma - (डिले'मऽ) **द्वि'शृंगिका /उभयापत्ती** : A situation in which one faces two or more mutually exclusive & mutually incompartible alternatives which are unsatisfactory & produces avoidance avoidance conflict.

diplopia - (डिप्लो'पिआ) **द्विदृष्टी** : double vision.

displacement - (डिस्प्ले'ऽस्म्न्ट) **विस्थापन** : a defence mechanism whereby a motive not expressed directly appears in a more acceptable form.

display rules - (डिस्प्ले' रूऽल्स) **शिष्टाचाराचे नियम, प्रदर्शन-नियम** : culture's rules for expression of emotions and ways of behaviour appropriate for situations.

dispositional attributions - (डिस्पझ़ि'शनल् ॲट्रिब्यु'शन) **व्यक्तिगत/ व्यक्तिसापेक्ष गुणारोपण** : deciding that other peoples actions are caused by their internal characteristics.

dissociation - (डिसो'ऽशिएऽशन्) **वियोजन** : spliting off psychological processes from rest of the personality.

distance cues - (डिं'स्टन्स क्यूज) **अंतराची नियामके** : the monocular and the binocular cues for the perception of distance.

distributed control - (डिस्ट्रि'ब्यूटेड कन्ट्रो'ऽल्) **वितरित नियंत्रण:** major functions of brain controlled by many different areas.

distributed practice - (डिस्ट्रि'ब्यूटेड प्रँ'क्टिस्) **वितरित सराव** : spacing of periods of practice over a period of time rather than massing the practice in one long learning session.

divergent thinking - (डायव्हऽजन्ट् थिन्किन्ग) **बहुदिश विचार** : creative thinking producing several solutions to a problem.

dizygotic twins - (डायझायगॉटिक व्टिन्स्) **द्विबीज, जुळी** : twins arising from two separate eggs i.e. fraternal twins.

dominant gene - (डॉ'मिनन्ट जीन) **प्रभावी जनुक** : member of a gene pair which determines a specific trait inspite of other member of the gene regardless of whether it is the same or different.

dopamine - (डोपामीन) **नससंवाहक** : a neurotransmitter of central nervous system.

double blind technique - (डबल ब्लाइन्ड् टेक्नी'क्) **उभयांध तंत्र** : experimental design where neither the investigator nor the patients know the treatment & nontreatment conditions during the experiment.

Down's syndrome - (डाउन्स सि'न्ड्रोम) **मंगोल लक्षण** : a form of mental deficiency produced by genetic abnormality due to extra chromosome on pair number 21.

draw a person test - (ड्रॉ अ प'ऽसन् टेस्ट्) **व्यक्तीचित्र रेखाटन कसोटी** projective technique for test of intellectual ability or mental retardation of children.

dream - (ड्रीम्) **स्वप्नानुभव** : imagery that occurs during sleep with coherent as well as bizarre aspect.

dream interpretation - (ड्रीम् इन्ट'ऽप्रिटे'ऽशन) **स्वप्नमीमांसा** : psychoanalytical technique analysing distinguished motives or symbolic meanings behind the dream.

dream-sleep - (ड्रीम्स्लीप्) **स्वप्ननिद्रा** : the rapid eye movement sleep.

dream wish - (ड्रीम् विश्) **इच्छामूलक स्वप्न** : the form in which repressed wish appears in a dream.

drive - (ड्राइव्ह) **प्रचोदना :** The motivational forces that make individuals active and lead them to pursue certain goal.

drive reduction theory - (ड्राइव्ह रिड'क्शन थि'अरी) **प्रचोदनाक्षयसिद्धान्त :** The theory states that the drive produced is weakened due to appropriate satisfaction of needs.

drug abuse - (ड्रग् अब्यू'स्) **घातकपरिणामी मादक द्रव्य सेवन :** improper use of drugs leading to serious consequences.

drug dependence - (ड्रग् डिपे'न्डस) **मादक द्रव्य अवलंबन :** compulsive drug use characterised by tolerance & withdrawal symptoms.

DSM - IV - (डी एस एम् फोर) **निदानात्मक आणि संख्याशास्त्रीय हस्तपुस्तिकेची चौथी आवृत्ती :** the fourth edition of the Diagnostic & Statistical Manual of American Psychiatric Association revised.

dual memory theory - (ड्यू'अल् मे'मरि थि'अरि) **दुपदरीस्मृतीउपपत्ती :** a theory that distinguished between short term memory and long term memory.

dual personality - (ड्यू'अल् प'ऽसनॅ'लिटी) **दुभंग/द्विविध व्यक्तिमत्त्व :** the simplest form of multiple personality.

duplicity theory - (ड्युप्लि'सिटि थि'अरी) **द्विस्तरउपपत्ती :** that rods & cones discharge dual visual function.

dynamic psychology - (डाइनॅ'मिक् साइकॉ'लजि) **मनोगतिक मानसशास्त्र :** concerned with motivation and with understanding causes of behaviour.

dyslexia - (डिस्ले'क्लिआ) **वाचनअक्षमता :** impairment of reading function. ∎

E

eating disorder - (ई'टिंग् डिसॉ'ऽडऽ) **क्षुधाविकृती** : a disfunctional relationship with food.

echoic store - (ए'कोऽक स्टॉअ) **श्राव्य-वेदनिक स्मृती** : a sensory memory lasting for a second or two following auditory stimulus.

eclectic approach - (इले'क्टिक् अप्रो'ऽच्) **बहुआयामी दृष्टिकोन** : an approach in psychology which draws on many different perspectives

ecological validity - (इकॉ'लजिकल् व्हॅलि'डिटि) **यथार्थता** : external validity

ectomorphy - (इक्टो'माऽफी) **मज्जाप्रधानता** : the characteristic of a person whose physique is dominated by outer skin and nervous system.

educational psychology - (ए'ड्युकेऽशनल् साइकॉ'लजि) **शैक्षणिक मानसशास्त्र:** the branch of psychology interested in application of psychological principles to the field education.

Edwards personal preference schedule - (एडवर्डस् प'ऽसनल् प्रे'फरन्स् शे'ड्युल्) **एडवर्ड वैयक्तिक प्राधान्य कसोटी** : a personality test useful for vocational guidance.

efferent - (एफ'ऽरन्ट) **कारक** : transmitting nervous impulses from the brain to muscles.

ego - (ई'गोऽ) **अहम् तत्त्व** : the conscious mind, one of three parts of mind in Freudian theory.

ego- ideal - (ई'गोऽ आय'डिअल्) **अहम् आदर्श** : part of superego which represents identification with parent figures who are admired.

eidetic image - (आयडिएटीक इमेऽज) **मूर्तिमंत/हुबेहुब प्रतिमा** : exceptionally vivid imagery of object, event or photographic image.

elaborative rehearsal - (इलॅ'बरे'ऽटिव्ह रिह'लसृल) **तपशीलवार विस्तारण उजळणी** : expanding verbal material to increase the ways to retrieve the material.

electra complex - (इले'क्ट्रा कॉ'म्प्लेक्स्) **पितृगंड** : the complex where a young girl desires her father and sees her mother as a rival.

electro convulsive therapy - (इले'क्ट्रो कन्व्ह'ल्सिव्ह् थे'रपि) **विद्युत-आघात पद्धती** : producing behavioral changes by passing an electrical current through patient's brain in treating severe depression.

electroencephalogram - (इलेक्ट्र'एनसेफ'लोग्राम) **मस्तिष्क विद्युतलेखी** : electrical brain potentials recorded via electrodes placed on scalp.

embedded figure - (इम्बे'डेड फि'गऽ) **अंतर्भूत आकृती** : a figure concealed within a more complex figure.

embryonic stage - (ए'म्ब्रिऑ'निक् स्टेऽज्) **भ्रूणावस्था** : the period of fertilized ovum from two weeks to two months when division of functions starts in different cells.

emotion - (इमो'ऽशन) **भावनानुभव** : a complex state of diffuse physical changes marked by strong feelings and accompanied by a behavioural impulse towards a specific goal.

emotional expression - (इमो'ऽशनल् इक्स्प्रे'शन्) **भावनाविष्कार** : the external (overt) behaviour that accompanies the emotional experience.

emotional intelligence - (इमो'ऽशनल् इन'टेलिजन्स) **भावनिक बुद्धिमत्ता** : the form of intelligence required for success in practical life dominated by emotional maturity.

emotional stability - (इमो'ऽशनल स्टॅबि'लिटि) **भावनिक स्थैर्य** : maturity and consistency in emotional behaviour.

empathy - (ए'म्पथि) **परानुभूती** : understanding another's point of view and sharing his emotions.

encephalitis - (एन'सेफ'लायटिस्) **मेंदूज्वर** : an inflammation of brain through infection disease.

encoding - (इन'कोडिन्ग) **संकेतन** : the transfer of information into code.

endocrine system - (एन्डो'क्राईन सिस्टम) **अंतःस्त्राव ग्रंथी संस्था** : system of ductless glands producing harmones.

endogamy - (एन्डोगॅमी) **सगोत्र विवाह** : restricting marriage partners to one's own kinship group.

endogenous depression - (एन्डोजीनअस डि'प्रेशन) **आंतरिक कारणोभ्दव खिन्नता विकृती** : depression resulting from internal biological causes.

endomorphy - ('एन्डोमॉर्फि) **स्थूलता/मंददेहिता** : fatty constitution.

endorphin - (एन्डॉ'फिन) **वेदनाशामक द्रव्य** : chemical produced by the body which acts like morphine to reduce pain.

engineering psychology - (ए'न्जिनि'अरिंग साइकॉ'लजि) **अभियांत्रिकी मानसशास्त्र** : Study of interaction between people their work environment.

engram - (एन'ग्रॅम) **स्मृतिचिन्ह/ठसा** : memory trace or physical representation of memory.

enuresis - (एन्युरेसिस्) **अनियंत्रित मूत्र विसर्जन** : involuntary release of urine, from emotional disturbance.

environmental psychology - (इन्व्हा'इअरन्मेन्टल् साइकॉ'लजि) **पर्यावरण मानसशास्त्र** : branch of psychology dealing with persons, environment, their interaction and resulting behaviour.

epilepsy - (ए'पिलेप्सि) **अपस्मार** : disturbances in the electrical activity of the brain caused by neurological disorder.

epinephrine - (एपि'नेफ्रीऽन) **एपिनेफ्रीन** : hormone secreted in response to stressful situations whose effects are similar to sympathetic division of autonomic nervous system.

episodic memory - (ए'पिसोऽडिक 'मेमरी) **घटना प्रसंगांची स्मृती** : memory of personal significance including circumstances in which a particular episode occurs.

ergonomics - (अग'नॉमिक्स) **मानव-यंत्र-संबंधशास्त्र** : study of interaction between people and their relationship to machines.

eros - (इ'रॉस) **जीवन प्रवृत्ती** : the self preserving drive for life.

escape learning - (इस्के'ऽप ल'निंग) **विमोचन अध्ययन** : learning to make a response in order to escape from an aversive event.

estrogen - (इ'स्ट्रजेऽन) **स्त्री-लैंगिक-ग्रंथी स्त्राव** : hormones chiefly produced by ovaries and responsible for most of the female secondary sex characteristics.

ethnocentricism - (इथनोसेन्ट्रीसीझम) **वंशवादी वृत्ती** : regarding one's own culture as more important.

ethology - (इ'थॉऽलजि) **नैसर्गिक निरीक्षणधारित, प्राणिजीवनाचा अभ्यास** : the study of animal behaviour in the natural environment.

euphoria - (यु'फॉऽरिअ) **हर्षोन्याद/उत्साहभरती** : abnormal sense of well being not based on reality.

evolutionary psychology - (ईव्हलू'शनरि साइकॉ'लजि) **उत्क्रांतीवादी मानसशास्त्र** : an approach which attempts to explain behaviour in terms of its functions & adaptiveness,

excitory neurotransmitter - (एक्सायटरी न्युरॉ'ट्रॅन्झिम'टऽ) **उत्तेजक नससंवाहक** : those which start functioning of neurons.

ex- post facto field study - (एक्स-पोस्ट फॅक्टो फीऽल्ड स्टि'डी) **घटनोत्तर क्षेत्रीय अभ्यास** : the field study which analyses the social behaviour after the event occurs.

exhibitionism - (एक्सिबि'शनिझम) **प्रदर्शन प्रवृत्ती** : a compulsion to expose oneself in public.

existential psychology - (इग्झि'स्टेन्शल साइकॉ'लजि) **अस्तित्ववादी मानसशास्त्र** : the view that task of psychology is to understand consciousness and contents of mind through immediate awareness.

exogamy - (एग्झॉ'गॅमि) **भिन्न गोत्र विवाह** : practice of restricting marriage partners to a person from out side one's kinship group.

exogenous - (इग्झॉजिनस) **बाह्य घटकाधारित** : based on the factors external to the organism.

experimental design - (एक्स्पे'रिमे'न्ट्ल् डिझा'इन) **प्रायोगिक आराखडा** : plan for collecting and treating the data of a proposed experiment.

experimental group - (एक्स्पे'रिमे'न्टल ग्रूप) **प्रयोग गट** : subjects in an experiment exposed to experimental variable.

experimental methods - (एक्स्पे'रिमे'न्टल् मे'थडस्) **प्रायोगिक पद्धती** : research designed to test cause effect relationships between variables.

experimental neurosis - (एक्स्पे'रिमेन्टल् न्युरॉ'सिस्) **प्रायोगिक विकृती** : disturbed behaviour of animals in an experiment when they are faced with confusing situation.

experimental psychology - (एक्स्पे'रिमे'न्टल् साइकॉ'लजि) **प्रायोगिक मानसशास्त्र** : the use of experimental methods to the study of psychological phenomena.

experimenter bias - (एक्स्पे'रिमे'न्टऽ बा'इअस) **प्रयोगकर्त्याचा पूर्वग्रह** : attempt by experimenter to influence outcome of experiment.

expert leader - (ए'क्स्पऽ ली'डऽ) **तज्ज्ञ नेता** : the leader who has a sound knowledge and can give perfect guidance to his followers.

expiatory punishment - (ए'क्सपिए'ऽटरि प'निश्मन्ट्) **सुसंगत शिक्षा** : the idea that the punishment should match badness of behaviour.

explicit learning - (इक्स्प्लि'सिट् ल'ऽनिन्ग) **उघड/हेतूपूर्वक अध्ययन** : a form of learning with a clear, definite purpose and voluntary effort.

explicit memory - (इक्स्प्लि'सिट् मे'मरी) **सुस्पष्ट स्मृती, व्यक्त स्मृती** : the conscious and explicit recollection of something.

external attribution - ('इक्स्टऽनल् ऑट्रि'ब्यूऽशन) **व्यक्तिबाह्य कारणिक गुणारोपण** : locating the cause of an event external to the person.

external validity - (इक्स्ट'ऽनल् व्हॅलि'डिटी) **बहिर्गत वैधता, यथार्थता** : the extent to which the findings of a research study are applicable to everyday situations.

extinction - (इक्स्टि'न्क्शन) **विलोपन** : disappearance of response if a conditioned stimulus is presented without usual reinforcement.

extra punitive - (ए'क्स्ट्रऽ प्यू'निटिव्ह) **पर-दंडनात्मक** : refering to blaming and punishing others in response to frustration

extra-sensory perception - (ए'क्स्ट्रऽ से'न्सरी प'सेप्शन) **अतींद्रिय संवेदनः** : ability to receive information about the world from sources other than the known senses.

extraversion - (ए'क्स्ट्रऽव्ह'ऽशन्) **बहिर्मुखता** : to be concerned with and derive gratification from the physical & social environment.

extravert - (ए'क्स्ट्रव्हऽट) **बहिर्मुखी (व्यक्ती)** : individual who displays extrovert behaviour.

extrinsic - (इक्स्ट्रि'न्सिक्) **बाह्य/बहिर्गत** : a feature that lies outside the organism.

extrinsic motivation - (इकस्ट्रि'न्सिक मोऽटिव्हेऽशन्) **बाह्य प्रलोभन प्रेरणा :** doing something for reasons of rewards or punishment external to the activity itself.

eye contact - (आइ कॉ'न्टॅक्ट्) **नेत्र-संबंध :** people looking each other in the eyes which indicates interpersonal distance & relationships.

eye-witness memory - (आ'इविट्निस् मे'मरि) **प्रत्यक्ष-दर्शी-साक्षीदाराची-स्मृती :** evidence supplied by people who witness a specific event or crime, relying only on their memory.

ethonesia - (इथोनेशिआ) **दयामरण :** the practice of mercy killing terminating in painless death.

■

F

F - scale - (एफ-स्केऽल) **अधिकारशाहीवृत्ती मापक श्रेणी** : a test of tendencies towards fascism.

fabulation - (फॅ'ब्युलेशन्) **अफलातून सत्याभासी कथाकथन** : telling fantastic stories deliberately as though they were true.

face to face group - (फेऽस् टू फेऽस् ग्रूप) **निकटसमूह** : small group with physical closeness to interact directly.

face validity - (फेऽस् व्हॅलि'डिटि) **दर्शनी वैधता** : the extent to which a psychological test appears relevant to the variable it is dealing with.

facial expression - (फेऽशल इक्स्प्रे'शन) **मुद्राविर्भाव** : the form of overt emotional expression appearing on the face of a person.

facilitation - (फसि'लिटेऽशन्) **सौकर्य** : easier performance of a given behaviour.

factor analysis - (फॅ'क्टऽ अनॅ'लिसिस) **घटक विश्लेषण** : a statistical procedure for analysing complex correlations of scores and tracing the factors underlying these correlations.

faith healing - (फे'ऽथ् ही'लिन्ग) **श्रद्धाधिष्ठित उपचार पद्धती** : attempt to heal sickness through non rational belief without medical means.

false consensus effect - (फॉ'ऽल्स् कन्से'न्सस् इफे'क्ट्) **आभासरूप सार्वत्रिक परिणाम** : a false belief that people think in the same way as one thinks.

false memory - (फाऽल्स मे'मरी) **मिथ्यास्मरण** : memory of a person, an object or event which is not experienced.

false memory syndrome - (फाऽल्स मे'मरि सि'न्ड्रोम) **मिथ्या स्मृती/असत्स्मृती संलक्षण** : recovering apparently repressed memories of events that did not happen.

family therapy - (फॅ'मिलि थे'रपि) **कुटुंब उपचार पद्धती** : probing disturbed relationships of family members for the treatment of observed individual neurosis.

fantasy - (फॅ'न्टसि) **दिवास्वप्न** : a deliberate act of imagination for one's wish fulfillment.

father figure - (फा'ऽदऽ फि'गऽ) **पितृतुल्य व्यक्तीमत्व** : someone who is seen as standing in place of one's real father.

fear of failure - (फिअ अव्ह फे'ऽल्यऽ) **अपयशाचे भय** : emotion aroused when a person feels pressure to achieve.

fear of success - (फिअ अव्ह सक्से'स्) **यशाचे भय** : a motive to avoid doing well and achieving success.

feeble mindedness - (फी'बल् मा'इन्डिड्नेस्) **मतिमंदता** : deficiency in mental ability.

feminity - (फे'मिनिटि) **स्त्रीसुलभ वैशिष्ट्ये** : characteristics peculiar to female sex.

feminism - (फे'मिनिझम्) **स्त्रीवाद** : a social movement committed to removal of prejudice against women, and their advancement.

feral child - (फेरल चाइल्ड) **पशुसंगोपित मूल** : a child reared by animals in the wild.

field experiment - (फील्ड् इक्स्पे'रिमन्ट्) **क्षेत्रीय प्रयोग** : a study in which the experimental method is used in a more naturalistic situation.

field theory - (फील्ड् थि'अरि) **क्षेत्रीय सिद्धान्त** : that brain is a total field and responds to totality of a field of interacting elements.

fight or flight response - (फाइट् ऑ फ्लाइट् रिस्पाँ'न्स्) **'लढा अथवा पळा' पलायन अथवा प्रतिकार प्रतिक्रिया** : the response made in the face of a threat, either resorting attacking or escaping behaviour.

figure & ground - (फि'गऽ ऑन्ड ग्राउन्ड्) **आकृती व आधारभूमी** : the pre- requisite for perception to take place is that the perceptual field is organised as figure distinguished against a relatively homogeneous back - ground.

fixation - (फिक्से'ऽशन) **कुंठितावस्था** : arrested development because of certain problems or excessive gratification.

fixed alternative test - (फिक्स्ट् ऑऽल्ट'नटिव्ह टेस्ट) **निश्चित पर्याय कसोटी** : test or questionnaire items that requires answer from a given selection of alternatives.

flash bulb memory - (फ्लॅश् बल्ब् मे'मरि) **लखख स्मृती** : a long lasting and vivid memory of a specific event and its context.

flooding therapy - (फ्लडिन्ग थे'रपि) **अंत:स्फोटक उपचार पद्धती** : behavioural therapy where maximum exposure is given to a feared stimulus until fear subsides thus extinguishing using a learned response.

fluid intelligence - (फ्लू'इड इन्टे'लिजन्स्) **प्रवाही बुद्धिमत्ता** : ability required for solving problem by abstract thinking.

focus of attention - (फोऽकस अव्क अटे'न्शन्) **अवधान केंद्र** : the object event or idea upon which one is concentrating.

foot in the door technique - (फुट् इन द् डॉऽस टेक्नी'क) **लघुत्तम महत्तम तंत्र/प्रवेश मान्यता तंत्र** : a larger request following a small request in a compliance technique.

forced choice technique - (फॉऽस्ड् चॉइस् टेक्नी'क्) **सक्तीच्या निवडीचे तंत्र:** a situation where one is required to choose one of the judgement although none is appropriate.

forensic psychology - (फरे'न्सिक् साइकॉ'लजि) **न्यायसाहाय्यक/न्यायवैद्यक मानसशास्त्र** : study of psychological factors in legal issues.

forgetting - (फगे'टिन्ग्) **विस्मरण प्रक्रिया** : the inability to recognise or recall information.

formal group - (फॉ'ऽमल ग्रूप) **औपचारिक समूह** : the group which is created and works on a certain set of rules.

formal operation stage - (फॉ'ऽमल ऑ'परे'ऽशन् स्टेज) **अमूर्त क्रियात्मक अवस्था** : last stage of development of child according to Piget in which the child becomes capable in abstract thinking.

forward conditioning - (फॉ'ऽवड् कन्डि'शनिन्ग) **पुरोगामी अभिसंधान** : a situation in which the conditioned stimulus is presented a short time before the unconditional stimulus, and remains while the unconditioned stimulus is presented.

fovea - (फो'विआ) **पीतबिंदू** : small area in the central part of retina, packed with cones, very effective in detail - vision & colour vision in daylight.

fraternal twins - (फ्रॅट'उन्ल् ट्विन) **बंधुभावी जुळी** : twins arising from two separate fertilised eggs.

free association methods - (फ्री असो'ऽशिएऽशन् मे'थड) **मुक्तसाहचर्य पद्धती** : psychoanalytical method to understand the unconscious mind by asking the client to say the first thing that comes into his or her mind.

free floating anxiety - (फ्री फ्लो'ऽटिंग् ऑन्झा'इअटि) **निराधार चिंता** : anxiety without a definite source and which can be attached to anything.

frequency - (फ्री'क्वन्सि) **वारंवारता** : number of times an event occurs in a study.

frequency distribution - (फ्री'क्वन्सि डि'स्ट्रिब्यूशन) **वारंवारिता वितरण** : a tabulation of the number of times something occurs in a study.

Freudian slip - ('फ्रॉइडीऽअन स्लिप) **चुकून निसटलेले शब्द** : mistake or substitution of words in speech or writing expressing hidden wishes or thoughts.

fringe incentives of benefits - (फ्रिन्ज् इन्से'न्टिव्ह बे'निफिट्स्) **आनुषंगिक प्रलोभने/लाभ** : the non-financial incentives given to the employees in the industries.

frustration - (फ्रस्ट्रे'ऽशन्) **वैफल्य** : blockage of goal directed behaviour or unpleasant state of tension.

frustration aggression hypothesis - (फ्रस्ट्रे'ऽशन् अग्रे'शन हाइपॉ'थिसिस्) **वैफल्य आक्रमकता अभ्युपगम** : an explanation for aggressive behaviour which states that frustration leads to aggression and aggression is always caused by frustration.

functional disorder - (फ'न्क्शनल् डिसॉ'ऽडऽ) **कार्यिक विकृती** : emotional disturbance which cannot be attributed to a physical cause.

functional fixedness - (फ'न्क्शनल् फिक्स्टनेस्) **साचेबंद समस्यापरिहार** : the tendency to solve a problem in a particular or fixed way.

functional MRI - (फ'न्क्शनल् एम आर आय) **कार्यात्मक एमआरआय** : using the MRI technology to study the brain in function.

functionalism - (फॅ'न्क्शनॅलिझम्) **कार्यवाद** : the school of psychology that emphasizes the function or activity of the mind rather than its content.

fundamental attribution error - (फॅ'न्डामे'न्टल् अॅट्रिब्यु'शन् ए'रऽ) **आरोपणातील मूलभूत प्रमाद** : tendency to overestimate the role of personal characteristics and to underestimate the role of situation.

G

Galvanic skin response - (गॅल्व्हॅनिक स्किन् रिस्पॉ'न्स्) **गॅल्व्हानिक त्वक् अनुक्रिया** : electrical reaction (in emotional situation) that can be detected by electrodes or the surface of the skin, (technique used in lie detector).

game theory - (गेम् थि'अरि) **क्रीडा उपपत्ती** : mathematical approach to the study of conflicts and decision making.

ganglia - (गॅन्ग'लिअ) **चेतागंडिका** : a group of neurons.

genaralised other - (जे'नलाइइड ॲ'दऽ) **अन्यजनसापेक्ष संकल्पना** : the concept an individual has of how other people expect him or her to behave in a given situation.

gender - (जे'न्डऽ) **लिंगप्रकार** : psychological characteristics associated with being male or female.

gender bias - (जे'न्डऽ बा'इअस्) **लिंगविषयक पूर्वग्रह** : differential treatment of men & women based on sterotypes rather than real differences.

gender identity - (जे'न्डऽ आइडे'न्टिटि) **लिंग तादात्म्य** : one's concept of being male or female.

gender role - (जे'न्डऽ रोऽल्) **लिंग संलग्न भूमिका** : the attitudes & behaviour appropriated to the gender.

gender stereotypes - (जे'न्डऽ स्टे'रिअटाइप्) **लिंगसंबंधी साचेबंद विचार** : the social perception of a man or woman based on belief about gender roles.

general ability - (जे'नरल् अबि'लिटि) **सामान्य क्षमता** : cognitive ability basic to all special or specific abilities.

general adaptation syndrome - (जे'नरल् अडप्टे'ऽशन् सि'न्ड्रोम) **सामान्य प्रतियोजन संलक्षण** : response to stress in three stages : alarm reaction, resistance and exhaustion.

general intelligence - (जे'नरल् इन्टे'लिजन्स्) **सामान्य बुद्धिमत्ता** : intelligence common to all normal individuals as basic ability.

generalised other - (जे'नरलाइड अॅ'दऽ) **लोकापेक्षेने निर्धारित स्वप्रतिमा** : the concept an individual has of how other people expect him or her to behave in a given situation.

general psychology - (जे'नरल् साइकॉ'लजि) **सामान्य मानसशास्त्र** : study of behaviour & mental processes applicable to humans and animals in general.

generativity - (जे'नरटिव्हिटी) **सर्जनात्मक क्रियाशीलता** : the development stage achieved in middle age according to Ericson, entailing ability to do creative work.

genes - (जीऽन्स्) **जनुके/रंगमणी** : units of inheritance that form part of chromosome.

genetic psychology - (जिने'टिक साइकॉ'लजि) **जननिक (विकास) मानसशास्त्र** : branch of psychology that studies behaviour by genetic method.

genetic method - (जिने'टिक् मे'थड्) **जननिक/वैकासिक पद्धती** : refers to explanation of behaviour in terms of hereditary origins & developmental history.

genital stage - (जे'निट्ल स्टेज) **मनोलैंगिक परिपक्वतेची अवस्था, लिंगनिष्ठ अवस्था** : the mature state of psychosexual development.

genius - (जी'न्यस्) **प्रतिभावंत** : the gifted person with IQ more than 180 and who stands above all intelligence tests.

genotype - (जीनोटाईप) **व्यक्तीची वंशाणुतील अव्यक्त शक्ती** : an individual's genetic potential.

gerontology - (जेरॉन्टॉ'लजि) **जराविज्ञान** : the study of old age and the process of ageing.

gestalt completion test - (गेस्टाल्ट कम्प्ली'शन टेस्ट्) **गेस्टॉल्टची चित्रपूर्ती कसोटी** : incomplete pictures which can only be completed correctly if the subject perceives the underlying unity and wholeness of picture.

Gestalt psychology - (गेस्टाल्ट साइकॉ'लजि) **समष्टीवादी मानसशास्त्र** : a school of psychology which insisted that psychological phenomena should be treated as 'gestalten' which could not be equated with elements which comprised them.

glial cells - (ग्लियल सेल्स) **आधार-पेशी** : cells that support and help for development of neurons.

glucostats - (ग्लू'कोऽस्टॅट) **रक्तशर्करामापक विशिष्ट पेशी** : specialised neurons in the brain and liver that measure the level of blood glucose.

goal directed behaviour - (गोल डिरेक्टेड बिहेव्ह्) **साध्यलक्षित वर्तन** : animal behaviour that can only be understood by assuming that it is intended to achieve a particular goal.

goal setting-theory - (गोल से'टिंग् थि'अरी) **साध्य-सापेक्ष प्रेरणा उपपत्ती** : a theory which suggests that motivation is raised by setting appropriate long - term incentives or goals.

gonad - ('गोनॅड) **लैंगिक ग्रंथी** : a sex gland.

graphology - (ग्रॅफॉ'लजी) **हस्ताक्षरविद्या** : study of handwriting .

grasping reflex - ('ग्राऽस्पिन्ग री'फ्लेक्स) **पकड प्रतिक्षेप** : the automatic response by fingers or toes in infants when the palm or sole of the foot is stimulated.

great man theory - (ग्रेट् मॅन थि'अरी) **विभूतीवादी उपपत्ती** : the idea that course of events is influenced at crucial times by the actions of outstanding individuals, a gross oversimplification in study of history.

gregariousness - (ग्रेगॅरीअसनेस) **कळपप्रवृत्ती** : tendency to live in flocks.

group dynamics - (ग्रूप डाइनॅ'मिक्स्) **समूह गतिकी/गतीविज्ञान** : study of ways people behave in groups.

group mind - (ग्रूप माइन्ड) **समूहमन** : a hypothetical entity supposed be responsible for crowd behaviour.

group morale - (ग्रूप मराऽल्) **समूह मनोधैर्य** : strong belief about group efforts and its success.

group norm - (ग्रूप नॉर्म्) **समूह मानदंड** : behaviour expected of all the members of a group.

group polorisation - (ग्रूप पॉ'ऽलराइझ़ेशन) **समूह ध्रुवीकरण** : the tendency of a group to become more exteme in its decision than its indidual members.

group socalisation theory - (ग्रूप सो'ऽशलाइझेशन थि'अरि) **समूह सामाजिकीकरण उपपत्ती:** the view that children are socialised by the groups outside home & the family.

group test - (ग्रूप् टेस्ट्) **समूह कसोटी** : a paper and pencil test given simultaneously to a large group of people.

group therapy - (ग्रूप् थे'रपि) **समूह उपचार पद्धती** : psychotherapy involving several people at the same time, and in which they are benefited by experiences of other people.

group think - (ग्रूप् 'थिन्क्) **समूह प्राधान्य** : excessive conformity to group opinion which is likely to lead to inappropriate action.

guilt culture - (गि'ल्ट कं'ल्चऽ) **अपराध भावना संस्कृती** : a culture that relies on its member's conscience and feeling of guilt to maintain order and social control.

gustation - (गं'स्टेऽशन्) **रुचिवेदन** : the sensation of taste.

■

H

habit - (हॅ'बिट्) **सवय :** a learned response to a given stimulus occurring almost automatically.

habitual attention - (हबि'ट्युअल अटेन्शन्) **सवयीचे अवधान :** the type of attention given to an object or event as a matter of habit i.e. quite automatically.

habituation - (हबि'ट्युएशन) **औषध सहिष्णुता / मादक द्रव्य सहिष्णुता :** psychological dependance on drug.

hallucination - (ह'लूऽसिने'ऽशन्) **अवस्तुभ्रम :** a perceptual illusion of a vivid experience which has no apparent reality in the external world.

hallucinogen - (हलू'सिनो'ऽजेन्) **अवस्तुभ्रमनिर्माणक :** psychoactive chemicals producing hallucinations.

halo effect - (हे'ऽलोऽ इफे'क्ट) **प्रभावलय प्रमाद :** the tendency for one outstanding trait to unduly influence an overall impression.

handedness - (हॅन्डेड्नेस्) **हस्तोपयोजन :** preference to use one hand or side of the body for certain activities.

handicapped - (ह'न्डिकॅप्ट) **अपंग :** a person with a congetinal or acquired mental or physical defect which interferes with normal functioning of the body.

hardiness - (हाऽ'डिनिस्) **कणखरपणा :** a clustor of traits possessed by those people best able to cope with stress.

Hawthorne effect - (हॅथॉर्न इफे'क्ट्) **हॅथार्न परिणाम :** tendency of people to work harder when experiencing a sense of participation, in something new & special.

health psychology - (हेल्थ् साइकॉ'लजी) **आरोग्य मानसशास्त्र :** branch of psychology dealing with psychological problems related to health.

healthy communication - (हे'ल्थि कम्यूऽनिके'ऽशन) **हितप्रद सुसंवाद** : the type of communication which is not only effective but also helpful in enhancement of better relationship.

hearing loss - (हि'अरिंग् लॉस्) **श्रवण-अक्षमता/बहिरेपणा** : degeneration of hearing ability caused by prolonged exposure to noise .

hedonism - (ही'डोनिझ्म) **सुखवाद** : our behaviour is motivated by a need to pursue pleasure and avoid pain.

hello goodbye effect - (हेलो'ऽ गु'ड्बाय् इफे'क्ट) **उपचारारंभी नाराज अखेरीस खुशमिजाज** : expressing unhappiness at the beginning and exaggerate well being at the end of the therapy.

hemispheres - (हे'मिस्फिअ) **(मेंदू) गोलार्ध** : the two halves of forebrain or cerebrum.

hemispheric asymmetry - (हे'मिस्फेरिक असिमे'ट्रि) **(मेंदू) गोलार्धातील असमानता** : imbalance between two cerebral hemispheres, where one is dominant for some behaviour.

heredity - (हिरे'डिटी) **अनुवंश/वंशदाय** : the biological transmission of characteristics from parents to offsprings.

hermaphrodite - (हऽमें'फ्रडाइट) **द्विलिंगी व्यक्ती प्राणी** : a person or animal with both the sex organs.

heroin - (हे'रोऽइन) **अफूजन्य मादकद्रव्य** : extremely addictive depressant derived from opium.

heterosexual bias - (हे'टरसे'क्शुअल) **भिन्न भिन्नलिंगी वर्तनविषयक पूर्वग्रहः** : the notion that heteroseuality is more natural and preferable to homosexuality.

heterosexuality - (हे'टरसे'क्शुऍ'लिटी) **भिन्नलिंगीय आकर्षण** : being attracted by the opposite sex.

heuristics - (ह्युअरि'स्टिक्) **नवगामी** : strategy that can be applied to variety of problems, usually yielding correct solution.

hidden observer - (हि'डन् अब्झ'ऽव्हऽ) **अदृश्य निरीक्षक** : in hypnosis a part of consciousness that is separate from the hypnotised self and remains more aware of what is happening.

hierarchy of needs - (हा'इअराऽकी अव्ह नीऽड्झ्) **गरजांची वर्चस्वश्रेणी** : classification of needs, ascending from basic biological needs to the highest human need for self actualization.

higher order conditioning - (व्हाइअऽ ऑं'ऽडऽ क'न्डि'शनिंग) **उच्च श्रेणीचे अभिसंधान :** a technique of classical conditioning in which previously established conditioned stimulus serves as the unconditioned stimulus.

hindsight bias - (हा'इन्डसाइट् बा'इअस्) **(घटिताच्या) पूर्वदृष्टीविषयी केलेला दावा :** tendency to believe that one knew all along what the outcome of an event would be.

holistic - (हो'लिस्टिक) **समग्र/सकल :** refering to whole of the behaviour and not its simplest units.

holophrasic period - **एकशब्द भाषा अवस्था :** first stage of language acquisition when children use holophrases, single words with complex meanings.

homeostasis - (होऽमीअ्'स्टेऽसिस) **समतोलत्व :** the process of maintaining a reasonably constant internal environment.

homosexuality - (होमो'ऽसे'क्शुअलिटी) **समलैंगिकता :** being attracted to people of the same sex.

horizontal vertical illusion - (हॉ'रिझॉन्ट्ल् व्हटिकल् इल्यू'झ्यन्) **लंब-क्षितीज भ्रम :** an optical illusion in which a vertical line appears to be longer than a horizontal line of equal length.

hormones - (हॉ'मोऽन्स्) **अंतःस्रावी ग्रंथी स्राव :** chemical substances produced by endocrine glands, and circulated in the blood.

horn - effect - (हॉर्न 'इफेक्ट) **नकारात्मक मिथ्यासामान्यीकरण :** judging a person from one negative characteristic to a total impression.

hostility motive - (हॉस्टि'लिटि मो'ऽटिव्ह्) **वैरभाव** motive involving enmity.

'hot-house' children - (हॉट्-हाउझ्-चिल्ड्रन) **कृत्रिम परिपक्वता लाभलेली मुले :** children whose intellectual capacities are artificially ripened.

human engineering - (ह्यू'मन् ए'न्जिनि'अरिंग्) **मानव अभियांत्रिकी :** study of relationship of people with machines & equipments.

humanistic psychology - (ह्यू'मनिस्टिक् साइकॉ'लजि) **मानव्यवादी मानसशास्त्र:** a psychological approach which emphasses uniqueness of human being, subjective experience and human values.

hunger derive - (हँ'नगऽ ड्राइव्ह्) **क्षुधाप्रेरक :** the drive based on food deprivation.

hydrocephalus - (हा'इड्रासेफॅलस) **जलशीर्षता :** excessive amount of cerebrospinal fluid within the skull resulting in enlarged skull and underdeveloped brain.

hydrophobia - (हाऽयड्रो'फोबिया) **जलभय :** symptom in humans of rabies, meaning, 'fear of water'.

hyperphagia - (हायपर'फेजिया) **अतिक्षुधन :** pathological overeating .

hyperthyroidism - (हायपरथा'इअरॉइडिझम्) **अतिक्रियाशीलता :** excessive secretions by thyroid gland that seem to cause heightened activity and exictement.

hypnosis - (हिप्नॉ'सिस्) **संमोहन :** an artificially induced sleeplike state in which the individual is highly suggestible to suggestions.

hypnotherapy - (हिप्नॉथे'रपि) **संमोहनोपचार :** a relaxation technique based on hypnotism to access the unconscious mind and memory store.

hypnotic trance - (हि'प्नॉटिक ट्राऽन्स्) **संमोहन-अवस्था/संमोहन तंद्री :** the dreamlike state of heightened suggestibility induced in a subject by a hypnotist.

hypochondria - (हाऽयपो'कॉन्ड्रिया) **रोगभ्रम :** the neurotic concern for one's health.

hypoglycemia - (हायपोग्लिसेमिया) **रक्तशर्करा न्यूनत्त्व :** deficiency of blood-sugar

hypomania - (हाइपॉ'मॅनिआ) **अल्पोन्माद :** mania or hyperactivity lasting for a short period of time.

hypovolumic thirst - (हायपो'व्हॉल्युमिक थस्ट) **रक्त आकारमान न्यूनताजन्य तहान:** thirst created by low blood volume.

hypothalamus - (हा'इपोऽ'थॅलमस्) **अधश्चेताक्षेपक :** located just above brain stem and below thalamus, this structure governs motivational behaviour, endocrine activity and maintains homeostasis.

hypothesis - (हाइपॉ'थिसिस्) **अभ्युपगम :** a verifiable statement based on certain theory.

hypnogenic stage - (हाइपोजेनिक स्टेज) **संमोहनजन्य अवस्था :** anything that helps to induce a state of hypnosis.

hysteria - (हिस्टि'रिअ) **उन्माद-विकृती :** neurosis, the product of unconscious conflict & emotional disturbances characterised by dissociation.

■

{ I }

iconic store - (आय'कॉनिक स्टॉऽ) **दृश्य-वेदनिक-स्मृती** : the image of visual stimulus which lasts very shortly in the memory.

Id - (इड्) **इदमात्मा/तदात्मा** : most primitive part of personality, consisting of basic biological imputes, according to Freud.

idealistic leader - (आइडिअलि'स्टिक् ली'डऽ) **आदर्शवादी नेता** : a typical leader who sticks to certain ideas and acts accordingly.

identical twins - (आइडे'न्टिक्ल् ट्विन्स्) **एकबीज जुळी** : twins derived from same fertilized ovum sharing hundred percent of their genes.

identification - (आइडे'न्टिफिकेशन्) **तादात्मीकरण** : changing ones attitudes & behaviour in order to be liked or admired by reference group.

identity - (आइडे'न्टिटि) **तादात्म्य/एकरूपता** : the basic unity of personality.

identity crisis - (आइडे'न्टिटि क्राइसिसिस) **स्व-तादात्म्य संघर्ष** : crisis due to the state of lacking a clear sense of what one is (as in adolescence)

idiographic approach - (आ'इडिओग्रॅ'फिक् अप्रो'च्) **व्यक्तिसापेक्ष दृष्टिकोन:** an approach which emphasizes the uniqueness of individual.

idiot - (इ'डिअट) **मूढतम/निर्बुद्ध** : a feeble-minded individual having an IQ less than 25, totally dependent on others in life-time.

idiot savant - (इ'डिअट् सॅ'व्हन्ट्) **विद्वन्मूढ** : scholarly idiot.

illusion - (इल्यू'झन्) **अपसंवेदन/भ्रम** : a mistake in perception due to physical or psychological reason.

imageless thought - (इ'मिजलेस् थॉऽट्) **प्रतिमारहीत विचार** : sequence of thoughts with no accompanying image.

imbecile - (इ'म्बिसाइल्) **दुर्बलमनस्क/मूढतर** : weak minded dependent on others, not educable but can control same basic life activities.

imitation - (इ'मिटे'ऽशन्) **अनुकरण** : copying another's behaviour.

immune system - (इम्यू'न सि'स्टम्) **प्रतिकार यंत्रणा** : a system of cells within the body that is concerned with fighting disease.

implicit learning - (इम्प्लि'सिट् ल'र्निंग्) **सुप्त-अध्ययन** : complex learning that occurs without the learner being able to verbalise.

implicit memory - (इम्प्लि'सिट् मे'मरी) **अबोध स्मृती, अव्यक्त स्मृती** : memory for previously learned activities or material that one apparently is not conscious of.

impression formation - (इम्प्रे'शन् फॉर्मे'शन्) **संस्करण-बिंबता** : the process by which one integrates various sources of information about another into an overall judgement.

impression management - (इम्प्रे'शन् मॅ'निज्मन्ट) **स्व-प्रभावाचे व्यवस्थापन:** attempt to present oneself to other people in such a way that they will react in a controllable or predictable fashion.

inkbolt test - ('इनब्लॉट टेस्ट) **शाईच्या डागांची चाचणी** : the test using inkblot pictures for the purpose of studying the projected motives & emotions of the subject.

incentive - (इन्से'टिव्ह) **प्रलोभन** : an external event or stimulus serving as reward in motivational behaviour.

incidental learning - (इ'न्सिडेन्ट्ल ल'निंग्) **अनुषंगिक अध्ययन** : learning which takes place with no apparent reinforcement.

independent variable - (इ'न्डिपे'न्डन्ट् व्हे'अरिअब्ल्) **स्वतंत्र परिवर्त्य** : the variable under experimental control.

individual differences - (इ'न्डिव्हि'ड्युअल् डि'फरन्सेस) **व्यक्ती भिन्नता** : dissimilarities in behaviour among members of same species.

individual test - (इ'न्डिव्हि'ड्युअल् टेस्ट्) **वैयक्तिक कसोटी** : the test which is administered to the individual alone for individual assessment.

induced motion - (इन्ड्यूस्ट मो'शन्) **प्रवर्तित गती** : the perception of motion of a stationary stimulus object produced by real motion of another stimulus object.

inductive reasoning - (इ'न्डे'क्टिव्ह री'झनिंग्) **विगामी विचारसरणी** : inferring general principles from specific examples.

industrial psychology - (इ'न्डे'स्ट्रिअल् साइकॉ'लजि) **औद्योगिक मानसशास्त्र:** branch of psychology concerned with selection, training, efficiency, evaluation and related problems of employees & employers in industries.

infancy - (इ'न्फन्सि) **अर्भकावस्था** : the stage of the newborn baby for a period of two weeks approximately.

infantile amnesia - (इ'न्फन्टाइल् ऑम्नी'झिअ) **शिशुकालच्या स्मृतीचा विसर** : loss of memory for events experiences that occured early in life.

infantile birth theories - (इ'न्फन्टाइल् ब'र्थ् थि'अराइझ्) **शिशुंनी जन्मविषयक केलेल्या कल्पना** : a young child's answer to the questions, 'where do babies come from?'

infantilism - (इन्फ'न्टिलिझम्) **बाल बुद्धीची अवस्था** : the condition of someone who has not developed psychologically beyond infancy or who regresses to that state when older.

inferiority complex - (इन्फि'अरिऑ'रिटि कॉ'म्प्लेक्स्) **न्यूनगंड** : feeling of inadequacy & resentfulness due to some defect.

informal group - (इन्फॉ'र्मल् ग्रूप) **अनौपचारिक समूह** : the group whose members are acting informally & with mutual understanding having no hard and fast rules.

information - (इ'न्फर्मे'शन्) **माहिती** : any stimulus with a mental content an image, idea, fact, opinion etc.,

information overload - (इ'न्फर्मेशन् ओ'व्हलो'उड्) **माहितीचा अधिभार** : the store of information beyond the capacity of processing it.

information processing - (इ'न्फर्मे'शन प्रसे'सिन्ग्) **माहिती संस्करण** : it is what happens between stimulus & response, according to cognitive psychology.

informational social influence - (इ'न्फर्मे'शनल् सो'श्ल् इन्फ्लुअन्स्) **माहितीच्या न्यूनत्वामुळे समूहापुढे झुकणे** : yielding to group pressure because others are thought to possess more knowledge.

informed consent - (इ'न्फॉ'र्म्ड् कन्से'न्ट्) **पूर्वकल्पनाधारित घेतलेली मान्यता** : a procedure by which people freely choose to participate in a study after they are told about the activities involved.

ingratiation - (इन्ग्रे'उशिएउशन्) **मर्जी संपादन तंत्र** : a technique used for compliance in an attempt to be liked by others.

ingroups - ('इनग्रूप्स) **अंत:समूह** : the groups to which individual belongs as against out groups.

inhibition - (इ'न्हिबि'शन्) **अडथळा/व्यत्यय/प्रतिबंध** : the blocking of one physiological or psychological process by another.

inhibitory neurotransmitter - (इन्हि'बिटरी न्यूरॉ ट्रॅन्झ्मि'टऽ) **अवरोधक नससंवाहक** : those neurotransmitters which obstruct functioing of neurons.

innate - (इने'ऽट्) **जन्मजात प्रवृत्ती** : a genetically inherited tendency that is present at birth.

insight learning - (इ'न्साइट् ल'ऽनिंग्) **मर्मदृष्टीचे अध्ययन** : a form of learning where a new behaviour is acquired through the sudden appearance of understanding.

insomnia - (इन्सॉ'म्निअ) **निद्रानाश** : dissatisfaction with the amount or quality of ones sleep.

instinct - (इ'न्स्टिक्ट्) **सहजप्रवृत्ती** : an innate impulse or motive.

institutionlisation - (इ'न्स्टिट्यू'शनलाझ्ऽशन्) **इस्पितळात / संस्थेत भरती करणे** : act of committing someone to an institution, such as mental hospital.

instrumental conditioning - (इ'न्स्टुमे'न्टल् कन्डि'शनिन्ग्) **साधनात्मक अभिसंधान** : a form of learning in which behaviour is controlled by giving of reward or punishment.

instrumental learning - (इ'न्स्टुमे'न्टल ल'ऽनिग्) **साधनात्मक अध्ययन** : a form of learning in which a behaviour becomes probable depending on its consequences.

intellectual leader - (इ'न्टले'क्ट्युअल् ली'डऽ) **बुद्धिवंत /विचारवंत नेता** : the leader who resorts to intellect and knowledge, rather than physical forces.

intellectualizing - (इ'न्टले'क्ट्युअलायझिंग्) **बौद्धिकीकरण** : dealing with situation in intellectual terms ignoring the emotion involved.

intelligence - (इन्टे'लिजन्स्) **बुद्धिमत्ता** : the ability to learn from experience, think in abstract terms and deal effectively with one's environment.

intelligence quotient (IQ) - (इन्टे'लिजन्स् 'क्वोऽशन्ट) **बुद्धिगुणांक** : a measure of general intellectual ability which can be calculated by dividing mental age by chronological age.

intelligence test - (इन्टे'लिजन्स टेस्ट) **बुद्धिमत्ता कसोटी** : the test that is supposed to measure intelligence.

interaction - (इ'न्टरॅ'क्शन्) **आंतरक्रिया** : mutually influencing actions between two individuals groups or individual and a group.

interference - (इ'न्टफि'अरन्स) **स्मृतीतील/अध्ययनातील व्यत्यय** : one kind of learning or memory inhibiting or disturbing another.

intermittent reinforcement - (इ'न्टऽमि'टन्ट् रीइन्फॉ'ऽस्मन्ट्) **खंडित, मध्यावधी, सान्तर** : intermittently rewarding an organism rather than continuously.

internal stimulus - (इ'न्ट'ऽनृल् स्टि'म्युलस्) **अंतर्गत उद्दिपक** : the stimulus arising out of physiological or psychological changes within an individual.

internal validity - (इ'न्ट'ऽनृल् व्हॅलि'डिटि) **सुसंगतता/अंतर्गत वैधता** : the validity of an experiment in terms of the context in which it is carried.

internalisation - (इ'न्ट'ऽनला'झेऽऽशन) **आत्मसातकरण/सात्मीकरण** : adhering to the ideas & values of the majority and accepting them thoroughly as ones own.

interpersonal attraction - (इ'न्टऽप'ऽसनल् अट्रॅ'क्शन) **आंतरवैयक्तिक आकर्षण** : attraction of people towards one another.

interpersonal conflict - (इ'न्टऽप'ऽसनल् कॉ'न्फ्लिक्ट्) **आंतरवैयक्तिक संघर्ष** : conflict between two persons.

interposition - (इ'न्टऽपझि'शन्) **अंशिक आच्छादन** : partially obscuring an object to provide a background cue for distance perception.

intervening variable - (इ'न्टऽव्हिनिन्ग् व्हे'अरिअबल्) **मध्यस्थ परिवर्त्य** : a hypothetical variable which is supposed to occur between a stimulus and response.

interview - (इ'न्ट'व्ह्यू) **मुलाखत** : a verbal research method in which the participant answers a series of questions

interviewer bias - (इन्टव्ह्यूअर बा'इअस्) **मुलाखतकाराचा पूर्वग्रह** : the effect on interview of conscious or unconscious biases of the interviewer.

intrapersonal conflict - (इन्ट्रॅ प'ऽसनल् कॉ'न्फ्लिक्ट्) **व्यक्तिअंतर्गत संघर्ष** : conflict within the person.

intrapunitive - (इन्ट्रॅप्यू'निटिव्ह) **दंडनात्मक** : refers to blaming and punishing oneself in response to frustration.

intrinsic motivation - (इन्ट्रि'न्सिक मो'टिव्हेऽशन) **आतंरिक प्रलोभन प्रेरण:** doing something for its own sake because the activity itself is rewarding.

introspection - (इ'न्ट्रस्पे'क्शन्) **आत्मनिरीक्षण** : observation and examination of one's own mental processes.

introspective method - (इ'न्ट्रस्पे'क्टिव्ह मे'थड) **आत्मनिरीक्षण पद्धती** : the method of obtaining information about mental processes by self observation and examination.

introversion - (इ'न्ट्रऽव्ह'ऽशन) **अंतर्मुखता** : basic personality dimension of being withdrawn & inward looking.

investigator effect - (इन्व्हे'स्टिगेऽटऽ इफे'क्ट) **संशोधनकर्त्याच्या अपेक्षांचा परिणाम** : the effect of investigator's expectations on the response of a participant.

involuntary attention - (इन्व्हॉ'लन्टरि अटे'न्शन) **अनैच्छिक अवधान** : a type of forced attention given to an object or event in spite of one's wishes or likes.

involution melancholia - (इन्व्हॉल्शन् मे'लन्को'ऽल्यऽ) **मध्यमवयीन खिन्नताविकृती** : a state of depression and anxiety associated with mid-life crisis in general.

Ishihara test - (इशिहारा टेस्ट्) **इशिहारा कसोटी** : a test for colour blindness.

∎

J

James Lange theory of emotions - (जेम्स लेंज थि'अरी अव्ह इमो'ऽशन्स) **जेम्स लेंज भावनाविषयक उपपत्ती** : a theory of emotions which suggests that emotion is our conscious awareness of bodily changes that follows an exciting event.

job analysis - (जॉब् अनॅ'लिसिस) **कार्यविश्लेषण** : study of elements of a job in an attempt to match the tasks assigned to the workers to their abilities.

job description - (जॉब् डिस्क्रि'प्शन्) **कार्यविवरण** : stating different elements of the job and relevant abilities required for it.

job placement - (जॉब् प्लेऽसमन्ट्) **कार्य-नेमणूक** : assignment of individual on the basis of job analysis.

job satisfaction - (जॉब् सॅ'टिस्फॅ'क्शन्) **कार्य-समाधान** : favorable attitude of the worker towards job conditions.

job specification - (जॉब् स्पे'सिफिके'ऽशन) **कार्य-निर्धारण** : description of a job and the requisite abilities needed for the success in the work involved.

Johari window - (जोहरी वि'न्डोऽ) **जोहरी (खिडकीचे) तंत्र** : a technique of counseling developed by Joseph & Harry (first names), psychologists considering mutual relations between the concerned person and another person.

just noticeable difference - (जेस्ट् नो'ऽटिसबल् डि'फरन्स्) **केवळ लक्षणीय भेद** : the minimum amount of difference that a subject can detect between two stimulus.

juvenile delinquency - (जू'व्हनाइल डे'लिन्क्वेन्सी) **बाल-गुन्हेगारी** : criminal behaviour committed by the children or adolescents. ■

डायमंड मानसशास्त्र - शब्दकोश । ५९

K

keyword technique - (कीवर्ड टेक्नी'क्) **शब्द-गुरूकिल्ली तंत्र, सूचक शब्द तंत्र** : the technique applied to aid memory in which some familiar word (keyword which is part of given word to be remembered) is associated with some visual image.

kinesthesis - (कायनेस्थेसिस) **स्नायुवेदन/आंतरवेदन** : the muscle tendon and joint senses.

kleptomania - (क्लेप्टोमॅनिया) **चौर्यकामुकता/अनिवार्य चौर्यप्रवृत्ती** : a compulsion to steal.

Korsakoff's syndrome - (कोर्साकॉफ्स् सि'न्ड्रोम्) **कोर्साकॉफचे संलक्षण** : a memory disorder involving amnesia, due mostly to alcoholism.

Kuder preference record - (कूडर प्रे'फरन्स् रे'कॉऽड्) **कूडर-प्राधान्य निवड कसोटी** : a questionnaire developed by Kuder designed to find out persons's vocational interest.

■

L

laboratory experiment - (लबॉ'रटरि इक्स्पे'रिमन्ट) **प्रयोगशालेय प्रयोग :** an experiment conducted in a laboratory setting, away from the participant's normal environment.

latency period - (ले'ऽटन्सी पि'अरिअड्) **सुप्तावस्था :** period between childhood and adolescence, when interest in sex is non-existent.

latent content - (ले'ऽटन्ट् कॉ'न्टेन्ट्) **(स्वप्नाचा) भावार्थ** the underlying meaning of a dream.

latent learning - (ले'ऽटन्ट ल'ऽनिंग्) **सुप्त-अध्ययन :** learning that takes place in the absence of any observable behavior.

lateral fissure - (लॅ'ट्रल् फि'शऽ) **पार्श्वखाच/सिल्व्हियसची खाच :** a deep fissure at the side of each of cerebral hemisphere also known as fissure of Sylvias.

lateral thinking - (लॅ'ट्रल् थिंकिंग्) **विविधांगी विचार :** a attempt to solve a problem by looking at it from various angles rather than head - on.

lateralisation - (लॅ'ट्रलायझेऽशन्) **विशिष्ट मेंदू गोलार्धातील स्थानिकीकरण** tendancy for neural functions to be located in some one hemisphere.

laterality - (लॅ'ट्रॅलिटि) **विशिष्ट बाजू अवलंबणे** sidedness

law of effect - (लॉ अव्ह् इफे'क्ट्) **परिणाम-नियम :** behaviour is repeated and strengthened followed by reinforcement, and weakened or extinguished in absence of reinforcement.

law of reinforcement - (लॉ अव्ह् री'इन्फॉ'ऽसमन्ट्) **प्रबलीकरणाचा नियम:** the probability of a response being produced is increased if followed by a reward or positive reinforcer.

laws of association - (लॉज् अव्ह् असो'ऽशिएऽऽशन्) **साहचर्य-नियम** : the principle underlying the connections in the memory between ideas, feelings & behaviour.

laws of learning - (लॉज् अव्ह् ल'ऽनिंग) **अध्ययनाचे नियम** : law of readiness, law of exercise and law of effect as formulated by Thorndike explaining trial & error learning.

leadership - (ली'ऽडऽशिप) **नेतृत्व** : a form of social influence where one member of the group alters the behaviour and thoughts of others with an intention to reach a goal.

leading question - (ली'डिंग् क्वे'श्न्) **सूचक प्रश्र** : the question asked to elicit an expected answer.

learned helplessness - (ल'ऽनिड् हे'ल्प्लिस्नेस्) **अध्ययनार्जित असहाय्यताः** passive behaviour on the part of the subject produced by the perception that punishment is unavoidable.

learning - (ल'ऽनिंग्) **अध्ययन** : a relatively permanent change in behaviour which is not due to maturation.

learning by trial & error - (ल'ऽनिंग् बाइ ट्रा'इअल् ॲन्ड् ए'रऽ) **प्रयत्न-प्रमाद - पद्धती** : the method of learning which is characteristic of skill acquisition where incorrect learning responses are reduced by practice & exercise.

learning curve - (ल'ऽनिंग् कऽव्ह्) **अध्ययन वक्र** : the curve obtained on graph by plotting measured changes in learning performance over time.

learning plateau - (ल'ऽनिंग् प्लॅ'टोऽ) **अध्ययनातील पठारावस्था** : the flattening of the learning curve due to temporary halt in learning progress.

learning set - (ल'ऽनिंग् सेट्) **शिकण्याचे तंत्र** : learning how to learn.

learning theory - (ल'ऽनिंग् थि'अरि) **अध्ययनाची उपपत्ती** : an attempt to explain the process of learning.

legitimate authority - (लिजि'टिमिट् ऑऽथॉ'रिटि) **सुयोग्य, वैध अधिकारः** the assumption about right of the people in power to tell others what to do because they have superior expertise, knowledge and ability.

lesbianism - (ले'स्बिअनिझम्) **स्त्रियांमधील समलिंगी संबंध** : female homosexuality.

level of aspiration - (ले'व्हल् अव्ह ॲ'स्पिरे'ऽशन्) **आकांक्षा पातळी** : the goals and standards of performance people set for themselves.

liberal humanism - (लि'बरल् ह्यू'मनिझम्) **उदार मानववाद** : the view that all people and their ways of conduct are basically equal.

libido - (लिबी'डोऽ) **(लैंगिक) ऊर्जाशक्ती** : psychic energy of the id, according to Freudian theory.

lie - detector - (लाइ-डिटे'क्टऽस) **असत्यशोधक यंत्रणा** : an instrument for monitoring physiological changes under conditions of emotional stress used as aid to detect criminal behavior.

life - instinct - (ला'इफ़् इ'न्स्टिन्क्ट्) **जगण्याची सहज प्रवृत्ती जिजीविषा** : an unconscious drive for preservation and enhancement of life.

life space - (ला'इफ़् स्पेऽस्) **जीवनावकाश** : totality of physical and psychological factors in the environement of an individual or group at any time.

life span - (ला'इफ-स्पॅन्) **जीवन-कक्षा** : the period between birth and death of an organism.

Likert scale - (लायकर्ट-स्केल) **लायकर्ट (अभिवृत्तीमापन) श्रेणी** : a three or fire point scale developed by Likert for measurement of attitudes.

Limbic Model - (लिंबिक् मॉ'ड्ल्) **लिंबिक प्रारुप** a physiological account of emotion identifying the brain structures involving lymbic system.

limbic system - (लिंबिक सिस्टिम) **किनारी संस्था** : a set of structures in and around the midbrain regulating motivational & emotional behaviour.

limen - (लिमेन) **सीमामूल्य** : threshold.

Lisergic acid diethylaminde (LSD) - (लायसर्जिक ॲसिड डायएथिलअमाईड) (एल.एस.डी) : a powerful psychoactive drug producing extreme alterations in consciousness, hallucinations & mood swings.

lobotomy - (लोबोटॉमी) **मेंदू अग्रखंड कर्तनशस्त्रक्रिया** : a type of psychosurgery, where frontal lobes are severed from the main part of the brain, formerly used to remove depression.

localisation - (लो'ऽकलाइझेऽशन्) **स्थानिकीकरण** : the view that certain areas of cerebral cortex are associated with specific behavioural functions.

locus of control - (लो'ऽकस अव्ह् कन्ट्रो'ऽल) **नियंत्रण केंद्र/स्थान** : personality dimension with which people attribute their experiences, either to forces within or external to themselves.

long term memory (LTM) - (लाँग् टऽम् मे'मरि) **दीर्घकालिक स्मृती** : a relatively permanent store of memory, which has unlimited capacity and duration.

longitudinal research - (लॉ'न्जिट्यूड्नल् रिस'ऽच) **अनुकालिक पद्धती** : a research method that studies an individual through time, taking measurements at periodic intervals.

loss aversion - (लॉ'स् अव्ह'ऽशन्) **नुकसानविषयक संवेदनशीलता** : greater sensitivity to losses than to gains.

lucid dreams - (ल्यू'सिड् ड्रीम्स) **सबोध स्वप्न, स्वयंनियंत्रित स्वप्न** : a dream where the individual is aware that he is dreaming and can sometimes control the dream content.

■

Machiavellian intelligence - (मॅकिअव्हे'लिअन् इन्टे'लिजन्स्) **कुटिल बुद्धिमत्ता:** the capacity to intentionally deceive another individual.

machine reductionism - (मशी'न् रिड'क्शनिझम्) **यांत्रिक वर्तनात्मक स्पष्टीकरण, यांत्रिक रूपान्तरवाद :** explaining behaviour by analogy with rather simpler machine system.

magic thinking - (मॅ'जिक् थिंकिंग्) **अतिमानवी विचार :** attempt to understand and manipulate human condition by recourse to super natural powers.

maladjustment - (मॅ'लड्जं'स्मन्ट्) **विषमायोजन :** inappropriate adjustment with the situation.

management games - (मॅ'निज्मन्ट गेम्स्) **व्यवस्थापन क्रीडा :** methods applied in management training for better skills & interpersonal relationships in industrial organisations.

mania - (मे'ऽनिअ) **उत्साहोन्माद विकृती :** uncontrollable excitement along with the impulse to perform a particular kind of behaviour.

manic depressive - (मॅ'निक् डिप्रे'सिव्ह्) **उत्साहोन्माद खिन्नता विकृती :** refers to extreme swings of moods from wild excitement of mania to deep depression.

mantra - (मंत्रा) **मंत्र :** a word or phrase repeated as an aid to meditation.

marasmus - (मरॅस्मस्) **कुपोषण :** severe physiological weakness found in infants suffering from deprivation of either food or love.

masking - (माऽस्किंग्) **आच्छादन :** blocking of one sensory process by another.

masnifest content - (मॅ'निफेस्ट कन्टे'न्ट्) **प्रगट आशय :** the actual or obvious contents of a dream, according to Freud.

masochism - (मॅ'सकिझ्म्) **आत्मपीडन :** the experience of sexual pleasure through suffering physical pain.

mass media - (मॅस् मी'डिअ) **जनसंपर्क/प्रसार-माध्यमे :** means of communication to the masses.

mass psychology - (मॅस साइकॉ'लजि) **जनसमुदाय-मानसशास्त्र :** study of behaviour of loosely organized groups or crowd behaviour.

massed practice - (मॅस्ड् प्रॅं'क्टिस्) **सतत/निरंतर सराव :** technique of learning in which lessons or periods of practice follow each other without a break.

mastery motive - (माऽस्टरि मॉऽटिव्ह) **स्वामित्व/प्रभुत्व प्रेरणा :** tendency to influence and dominate & exercise power over others.

matched pairs design - (मॅचऽ पेअऽस् डिझा'इन) **अनुरूप युग्म आराखडा :** a research design where participants are matched on one to one basis and not as a whole group.

matching hypothesis - (मॅचिन्ग् हाइपॉ'थिसिस्) **समरूप आकर्षण अभ्युपगम:** the notion that we are attracted to those who are about as physically attractive as we are.

maternal drive - (मट'ऽनल् ड्राइव्ह्) **मातृत्व-प्रेरक/वात्सल्यप्रेरक :** a drive induced in female through bearing, nursing and caring for the young.

matriarchy - (मॅ'ट्रिआऽकी) **महिलाधिष्ठित समाज :** a society run by women.

maturation - (मॅ'च्युरेऽशन्) **परिपक्वन :** process of growth and development common to all members of a species irrespective of individual heredity & environment.

maze - (मेऽझ्) **व्यूह :** an instrument designed for learning experiments.

mean - (मीन्) **सरासरी :** the number obtained by dividing total of participants' scored by number of participants.

mechanical aptitude test - (मेकॅ'निकल ऍप्टिट्यूड् टेस्ट्) **यांत्रिक अभिक्षमता चाचणी :** test for evaluation of ability to deal with mechanical devices and to understand mechanical relationships.

median - (मी'डिअन्) **मध्यमान :** the middle score out of all participants' scores when data have been put into numerical order.

mediator codes - (मी'डिएऽटऽ को'डस्) **मध्यस्थ संकेत :** the non verbal communication codes based on intermediary means like pictures, graphs, slides etc.

medical model - (मे'डिकल् मॉ'ड्ल्) **वैद्यकीय प्रारूप** : model with a medical approach to treat illness.

meditation - (मे'डिटे'ऽशन्) **ध्यान** : an altered state of consciousness in which individual is extremely relaxed 'divorced from outside world' & enters wider consciousness.

megalomanic - (मे'गलो'ऽमे'ऽन्यक्) **स्वयंमन्य-महानता उन्माद** : a mania for oneself having exaggerated view about ones abilities and improtance.

melancholia - (मे'लन्को'ऽल्यऽ) **विषण्णता** : melancholy mood, characterized by sadness and severe depression.

melatonin - (मेलॅ'टॉनिन) **निद्रापक ग्रंथिस्राव** : a harmone produced by pineal gland that increases sleepiness.

membership group - (मे'म्बऽशिप ग्रूप्) **सदस्यता समूह** : a group to which an individual belongs.

memory - (मे'मरि) **स्मृती** : the mental processes which are used to encode, store and retrieve information.

memory drum - (मे'मरि ड्रम्) **स्मृति दंडगोल** : a common laboratory equipment (drum) which presents a series of stimulus to a subject for memory experiments.

memory span - (मे'मरि स्पॅन्) **स्मृति-विस्तार** : the number of items a subject can recall after single presentation of material .

memory trace - (मे'मरि ट्रेऽस्) **स्मृती ठसा / अवशेष** : the supposed neurological events which are responsible for any relatively permanent memory.

mental age - (मे'न्टल एऽज्) **मानसिक वय** : the score on intelligence test where items are graded by difficulty and standardised against chronological age.

mental health - (मे'न्ट्ल् हेल्थ्) **मानसिक आरोग्य** : a state of good adjustment with a subjective state of well being. The concept of mental health involves physiological, psychological and social dimensions.

mental retardation - (मे'न्ट्ल् रिटा'ऽडेशन्) **मानसिक मंदत्व** : technically used term to denote people below 70 IQ.

mental set - (मे'न्टल् सेट्) **मानसिक सज्जता** : readiness for a particular experience.

mental test - (मे'न्ट्ल् टेस्ट्) **मानसिक कसोटी** : any test which is designed to evaluate a specified mental ability or performance.

mesmerism - (मे'झमरिझम्) **मोहिनीप्रयोग** : early name for hypnosis named after Franz Mesmer.

meta analysis - (मेटॅ'अनॅ'लिसिस्) **अतिविश्लेषण** : an analysis where all findings from various studies about a given subject are combined for statistical testing.

meta psychology - (मे'टॅ साइकॉ'लजि) **अतिमानसशास्त्र** : attempt to go beyond existing theory and observations and speculate about the human behaviour in general.

method of constant stimuli - (मे'थड् अव्ह् कॉ'न्स्टन्ट स्टि'म्युली) **स्थिर उद्दिपक पद्धती** : a psychophysical method for determining sensory thresholds.

method of Loci - (मे'थड अव्ह् लोसी) **स्थान-संबंध पद्धती** : aid to serial memory where verbal material transformed to mental images is located at successive positions along a visualised route.

micro sleep - (मा'इक्र स्लीप) **अल्पकालीन निद्रासदृश शिथिलावस्था** : brief periods of relaxed wakefulness during the day.

middlescence - (मि'ड्ल्सेन्स) **मध्यमवयीन ताणतणाव** : stresses and conflicts of middle age and its positive aspects.

milieu therapy - (मी'लिअ थे'रपि) **परिस्थिती परिवर्तनाधारित उपचारपद्धती:** a psychotherapy focusing on helping people by changing their enviornment.

military psychology - (मि'लिटरी साइकॉ'लजि) **सैनिकी-मानसशास्त्र** : branch of applied psychology dealing with the problems related to life in armed forces, especially with its psychological aspect.

minimax strategy - (मि'निमॅक्स् स्ट्रॅ'टिजि) **हानी-लघुकारक वर्तन प्रयुक्ती** : a strategy of choosing to minimise loss rather than maximising.

minority influence - (माइनॉ'रिटि इन्फ्लुअन्स्) **अल्पसंख्याकाचा प्रभाव** : a majority being influenced to accept the beliefs or behaviour of a minority.

mirror writing - (मि'रऽ रा'इटिन्) **दर्पण लेखन** : writing that is reversed but appears as normal when seen in a mirror.

misanthropic - (मि'सन्थ्रोपिक) **मनुष्यद्वेष्टा** : hating other people.

mnemonics - (निमॉ'निक्स) **स्मृती-साहाय्यक-तंत्रे** : tricks to aid the memory.

mob - (मॉब) **झुंड** : crowd of individuals acting under strong emotional conditions leading to violence.

modality - (मॉ'ड्लिटि) **विशिष्ट वेदनप्रकार** : particular form of sensory experience.

mode - (मोऽड) **बहुलक** : the most frequently occurring score among participants' scores in a given condition.

modelling - (मॉ'ड्लिन्ग्) **प्रतिरूप अनुसरण** : observing a model and imitating the behaviour.

monochromatism - (मॉ'नक्रॉऽमॅटिझम्) **पूर्ण-रंगांधत्व** : a rare disorder which involves total colour blindness.

monocular cues - (मॉ'नक्युलर क्यूज्) **एकनेत्र नियामके** : cues to depth perception that require the use of only one eye.

monozygotic twins - (मॉ'नझायगॉ'टिक् व्टिन्स्) **एकबीज जुळी** : indentical twins derived from same fertilised ovum.

mood - (मूड) **भावस्थिती/मनस्थिती** : a transitory state of emotion.

motherse - (मदसे) **बालसुलभ मायबोली** : a special style of speaking used by mothers when talking with children.

motion after effect - (मो'ऽशन् आ'ऽफ्टऽ इफे'क्ट) **गतीवेदनाचा पश्चात परिणामः** the illusion of movement in a static object in opposite direction to viewed motion which occurs after viewing motion for an extended period of time.

motion parallax - (मो'ऽशन् पॅ'रलॅक्स्) **विरोधी-गती/सापेक्ष गती** : a visual cue of depth perception based on the fact that things which are closer move faster in relation to things that are further away.

motivated forgetting - (मो'ऽटिव्हेऽटेड फगे'टिन्ग्) **प्रेरित विस्मरण** : psychoanalytical interpretatin of forgetting : forgetting occurs due to "motive to forget" certain unwanted and painful events which leads to repression of them.

motivation - (मो'ऽटिव्हेऽशन्) **प्रेरणा** : experiencing of needs and drives and the behaviour that leads to the goal which satisfies them.

motivational cycle - (मो'टिव्हेऽशनल सा'इक्ल्) **प्रेरणा चक्र :** the cycle or activities starting from creation of need to need satisfaction through relevant goal-directed efforts.

motor learning - (मो'टऽ ल'ऽनिंग्) **कारक अध्ययन :** learning related to skills that require muscle coordination.

movement error - (मू'व्हमन्ट् ए'रऽ) **गतिप्रमाद :** error committed when an instrument is moved in one direction only.

Muller-Lyer illusion - **म्युलरलायर - भ्रम :** a distorted visual perception of length where two straight lines of same length between the arrows enclosed differently appear to be of different lengths.

Multistore model - (मेल्टिस्टॉऽ मॉ'ड्ल्) **बहुप्रकार साठवणस्मृती प्रारूप :** the concept that memory is divided into several kinds of stores namely sensory, short terms and long-term.

multiple approach-avoidance conflict - (मे'ल्टिपल अॅप्रो'ऽच् अव्हॉ'इडन्स् कॉन्फ्ल'क्ट्) **बहुविध प्रगमन - वर्जन संघर्ष :** the psychological conflict which arises when there are more than one object / goal before the person, which are both attractive and repulsive at the same time.

multivarient experiment - (मे'ल्टि व्हॅ'रिअन्ट् इक्स्पो'रिमन्ट्) **बहुघटक प्रयोग:** a type of experiment involving simultaneous manipulation of several independent variables.

myogram - (माइऑ'ऽग्रॅम) **स्नायुक्रिया आलेख :** the graphic representation of muscular activity.

myopia - (माइऑ'ऽपिअ) **दीर्घदृष्टिदोष :** nearsightedness.

myxedema - (मिक्सिडीऽमा) **क्रियाक्षीणता :** condition of severe depression of nervous system activity characterised by lethargy arising out of thyroxin deficiency.

naive participant - (नाऽई'ड्व् पाऽ'टिसिपन्ट) **नवखा प्रयुक्त :** a participant who is unfamiliar with the experiment, or who has been misled as to the real purpose of the experiment.

narcissism- (ना'ऽसिसिझ्म्) **आत्मरती (आत्मप्रीति) :** excessive self-love characterized by a preoccupation with one's self to the exclusion of others.

Narco - therapy - ('नाऽको थेरपी) **सुषुप्ती उपचार पद्धती :** any therapy that makes use of narcotic drug.

narcolepsy - (नाऽकॉ'लेप्सी) **अचानक झोपेची तंद्री/डुलकी :** a disease characterised by an uncontrollable need to sleep.

narcosis - (नाऽकॉ'सिस) **प्रतिसाद क्षीणत्वाची अवस्था :** a state of markedly reduced responsiveness, both in behaviour and normal physiological functioning, induced by narcotic drug.

narcotics - (नाऽकॉटिक्स्) **शांतक व वेदनाहारक औषधी :** any drug that has both sedative and analgestic properties.

nativism - (नटि'व्हिझम्) **अनुवंशवाद :** the view that characteristics are inherited.

natural experiment - (नॅ'चरल् इक्स्पे'रिमन्ट्) **नैसर्गिक प्रयोग :** a type of experiment (a quasi - experiment) where use is made of some naturally occurring independent variable.

naturalistic observation - (नॅ'चलिस्टिक् अब्झ'ऽव्हेशन) **नैसर्गिक निरीक्षण:** an objective observational study conducted in a natural setting.

nature nurture debate - (ने'ऽचऽ न'ऽचऽ डिबे'ऽट्) **निसर्ग संगोपन वाद/ सृष्टी-पुष्टी वाद :** the question of whether behaviour is determined solely by heredity or by environment.

need - (नीड्) **गरज** : a physical state involving any lack or deficit within the organism.

need for achievement - (नीड् फॉऽ अची'व्हमन्ट्) **संपादनाची गरज** : the strongly felt motivation to achieve, to accomplish ambitions to be successful.

need for affiliation - (नीड् फॉऽ अफि'लिए'ऽशन) **सहवास गरज** : the need to be with other people, particularly when facing same unpleasant experience.

need reduction - (नीड् रिड'क्शन्) **गरज-क्षय** : diminishing of a need in the course of motivational cycle.

negative after image - (ने'गटिव्ह आ'ऽफ्टऽ इ'मिज्) **ऋण पश्चात प्रतिमा:** an after image whose properties are antagonistic to original stimulus.

negative correlation - (ने'गटिव्ह कॉ'रिले'ऽशन) **ऋण-सहसंबंध** : the variation in constant relationship of two variables where one covariable increases the other decreases.

negative incentive - (ने'गटिव्ह इन्से'न्टिव्ह) **ऋण प्रलोभन** : the object away from which behaviour is directed in motivational process.

negative reinforcement - (ने'गटिव्ह री'इन्फॉ'ऽस्मन्ट्) **ऋण-प्रबलीकरण:** in conditioning process, it is the rewarding of an act that ends unplesant state.

negative self-concept - (ने'गटिव्ह सेल्फ् कॉ'न्सेप्ट्) **नकारात्मक स्व संकल्पना:** individual's unfavorable self-image about himself or herself.

negative transfer - (ने'गटिव्ह ट्रॅ'न्स्फऽ) **ऋण (अध्ययन) संक्रमण** : the detrimental effect of pervious learning on later learning.

neo - behaviorism - (नी'ओ बिहे'व्हरिझम्) **नव-वर्तनवाद** : an extension of behaviorism to allow for some cognitive factors.

neo dissociation theory - (नी'ओ डिसो'ऽशिएऽएशन् थि'अरी) **नव-वियोजन उपपत्ती** : the theory which states that one part of the mind is separated off from the other parts in hypnotic state.

neologism - (नीओ'लजिझम्) **नवीन शब्दार्थरचना** : creating alternative new phrases or attaching new meaning to current words & phrases.

nervous breakdown - (न'व्हस् ब्रेऽक्डाऽउन्) **चेतावभंजन** : severe neurosis which incapacitates an individual and requires hospital treatment.

nervous disorder - (न'व्हस् डिसॉ'ऽडऽ) **चेतीय विकृती (नसविकृती):** a functional psychological disorder with no organic causes which can be properly dealt with by psychotherapy.

neurologist - (न्यूरॉ'लजिस्ट्) **चेतावैज्ञानिक :** the scientist who is expert in neurology i.e. science of structure and function of nervous system.

neuro transmitter - (न्यूरॉ'टॉन्झिम'टऽ) **नस-संवाहक :** a chemical substance released at the junction between neurons and which effects the transmission of messages in nervous system.

neuropsychology - (न्यूरॉ'साइकॉ'लजि) **नस-मानसशास्त्र :** the branch of psychology concerned with the relationship between nervous system, mental processes & behaviour.

neuropyschiatry - (न्यूरॉ'साईका'इअट्रि) **नस-मानसविकृतीशास्त्र :** branch of medicine which deals with the relationship between neural processes and psychiatric disorders.

neurosis - (न्यूरॉ'सिस) **वैकल्य नसविकृती :** a functional psychological disorder with no organic causes which is dealt with by psychotherapy.

neurotic anxiety - (न्यूरॉ'टिक् ॲन्झा'इअटि) **नस-चिंताविकृती :** fear that is out of proportion to the actual danger posed.

night blindness - (नाइट् ब्लाइन्डनेस) **रातांधळेपणा :** a weakened capacity for dark light adaptation due to organic disease or vitamin deficiency.

night terror - (नाइट् टे'रऽ) **भयंकर स्वप्न :** the type of dream experienced in non-rem-sleep in which the person is terribly frightened by a series of calamities and gets awakened in a fearful state with shouting and screaming

nightmare - (नाइटमेअ) **भयस्वप्न :** the type of dream experienced in REM sleep in which the person is frightened by some calamity and gets awakened in a fearful state.

nomothetic approach - (नॉम्अथेटिक अप्रो'उच)**नियमसापेक्ष दृष्टिकोन :** an approach based on attempt to establish general laws of behaviour.

non declarative memory - (नॉ'न्डे'क्लरे'ऽटिव्ह मे'मरि) **अवाचक/प्रक्रियाधारित स्मृती :** memory related to specific skills, habits and related information.

non directive therapy - (नॉ'न्‌ड़िरे'क्टिव्ह थे'रपि) **विना-निर्देशन-मानसोपचार पद्धती** : the therapy which depends on individuals expression of his problems in his own terms without any interpretation and which does not lead him to a particular direction.

non language test - (नॉन्‌ लँ‌न्‌ग्विज् टेस्ट्) **अभाषिक कसोटी** : test using concrete, non verbal materials.

non sense syllables - (नॉ'न्‌सन्स् सि'लबल्) **निरर्थक शब्दबंध** : three letter combinations (like ZEJ) which have no meaning for the participant, and which are used in the studies of memory.

non- rem sleep - (नॉनरेम् स्लीऽप) **जलद नेत्र-हालचाल न होणारी झोप** : refers to those stages which are not characterised by rapid eye movements.

non verbal communication - (नॉन् व्हऽबल् कम्यू'निके'ऽशन) **अशाब्दिक संप्रेषण** : direct communication between people by means other than spoken words.

non-educable - (नॉन् ए'ड्‌युके'ऽबल्) **अनध्यापनीय** : persons who cannot be educated in the conventional sense.

norm - (नॉऽम्) **वर्तनाचा मानदंड** : cultural expectations, standards of behaviour.

norm of reciprocity - (नॉऽम् अव्ह रिसिप्रॉ'सिटी) **जशास तसे वर्तन** : the cultural expectation that it is justified to treat others in the way they treat you.

normal - (नॉ'ऽमल्) **प्रसामान्य** : confirming to the norm a standard.

normal distribution - (नॉ'ऽमल् डि'स्ट्रिब्यूशन्) **घंटाकार प्रसामान्य वितरण:** the bell shaped distribution of data in which most of the scores are close to the mean.

normative social influence - (नॉ'ऽमटिव्ह सॉ'शल् इन्फ्लुअन्स्) **प्रशंसापेक्षी अनुसरिता** : confirming others in order that others will like or respect oneself.

nuclear family- (न्यू'क्लिअ फँ'मिली) **विभक्त परिवार / आण्विक परिवार** : mother, father and two - three children.

null hypothesis - (नॅल् हाइपॉ'थिसिस्) **यदृच्छाधारित संशोधन अभ्युपगम्** : a hypothesis that any findings are due to chance factors and do not reflect true relationship.

O

obesity - (ऑबी'सिटि) **स्थूलत्व/लठ्ठपणा** : disorder caused by over - eating.

object assembly : (ऑब्जिक्ट असे'मब्लि) **वस्तू-जुळवणी कसोटी** : a test where the subject is asked to put together disassembled object

object cathexis - (ऑब्जिक्ट कॅथेक्सिस्) **लैंगिकेतर प्रेमवस्तु** : choice of a love object, usually non-sexual object.

object constancy - (ऑब्जिक्ट कॉन्स्टन्सि) **वस्तुसातत्य** : the experience that the familiar objects are perceived in the same manner regardless of changes in the environment.

object permanence - (ऑब्जिक्ट प'उमनन्स्) **वस्तुनित्यता** : an awareness in young children that objects continue to exist when they can no longer be seen.

observer bias - (अब्झ'उव्हउ बा'इअस्) **निरीक्षकाचा पूर्वग्रह** : effect of prejudices or expectations of the observer on the things observed.

observer effect - (अब्झ'उव्हउ इफे'क्ट) **निरीक्षकाचा परिणाम** : unnatural behaviour that is produced when someone is observing.

observational learning - (ऑब्झव्हे'उशनल् ल'उनिंग्) **निरीक्षणात्मक अध्ययन:** the form of learning based on copying or observing the behaviour of others.

observational method - (ऑ'ब्झव्हे'उशनल् मे'थड्) **निरीक्षणात्मक पद्धती** : studying events as they occur in nature without experimental control of variables.

obsession - (अब्से'शन्) **पछाडणारा विचार/कल्पना अनिवार्यता** : a persistent anxiety - provoking idea that one cannot get rid of .

obsessive compulsive neurosis - (अब्से'सिव्ह् कम्प्'ल्सिव्ह् न्युरॉ'सिस्) **कल्पनाक्रिया अनिवार्यता विकृती :** a neurosis in which an individual is not only obsessed by certain idea but feels compelled to act on them, ritually and repetitively.

obstruction method - (ऑबस्ट्र'क्शन् मे'थड्) **अडथळ्याची पद्धती :** a technique used for measuring the relative strength of animal drives by puting one against another.

occipital lobe - (ऑक्सिपिट्ल लोब) **पार्श्वखंड/पृष्ठखंड :** region at the back of the brain that processes visual infromation.

occupational psychology - (ऑक्युपे'उशनल् साइकॉ'लजि) **व्यावसायिक मानसशास्त्र :** the branch of psychology concerned with occupational selection, training and particularly occupational adjustment.

occupational therapy - (ऑ'क्युपे'उशनल् थे'रपि) **व्यवसाय-मानसोपचार पद्धती :** involving patients in performing useful tasks to improve their self-esteem and feelings of worth, and physical condition as well.

oedipus complex - ('इडिपस कॉ'म्प्लेक्स) **मातृगंड :** the Freudian notion that the young boys desire their mother sexually and so experience rivalry with their father.

olfaction - (ऑल'फॅक्शन) **गंधवेदन :** the sense of smell

on the job-training - (ऑन द जॉब ट्रेउनिंग) **प्रत्यक्ष कार्यसमवेत प्रशिक्षण :** training given while doing the job.

one - trial learning - (वन्-ट्रा'इअल् ल'उनिंग्) **एकपाठी अध्ययन :** learning that occurs after a single trial or practice.

one way screen - (वन-वेउ स्क्रीउन) **एकदर्शी पडदा :** a window into a room that looks like a mirror to the participant on the other side.

open ended question - (ओउपन-एन्डिड क्वे'श्न्) **खुला प्रश्न :** any question in questionnaires which a subject is allowed to answer in his own way.

open group - (ओउपन ग्रूप) **खुला ग्रुप :** the group whose membership is open to anybody who wishes to join.

operant behaviour - (ऑ'परन्ट् बिहे'उव्हार) **साधनात्मक/व्यापारात्मक वर्तन :** instrumental behaviour.

operant conditioning - (ऑ'परन्ट् कन्डि'शनिंग्) **साधनात्मक अभिसंधान :** a form of learning in which behaviour is controlled by giving of reward or punishment.

operational diagnostic criteria- (ऑ'परेऽशनल डाइअग्नोऽस्टिक् क्राइटि'अरिअ) **क्रियात्मक निदान निकष :** a set of standards used to judge whether someone is suffering from a particular mental illness.

opiates - (ऑऽपिअट्स्) **अफूजन्य मादक पदार्थ :** highly addictive chemical depressant which relieves pain & produces euphoria.

opinion leader - (अपि'न्यन् 'लीऽडअ(र)) **विचारवंत/मतपरिवर्तनकारी नेता:** a person whose opinions are highly thought of and who can therefore influence the opinions of other members.

opponent colour theory - (अपॉ'नन्ट् कं'लऽ थि'अरि) **रंगविषयक विरोधी प्रक्रिया उपपत्ती :** colour perception theory which postulates two types of colour sensitive units that respond in opposite ways to the two colours of opposite pairs.

optic nerve - (ऑप्टिक् नऽव्ह्) **दृष्टिनस :** in vision, the nerve formed out of axons of ganglion cells, leading to the brain.

optimum level of arousal - (ऑ'प्टिमम् ले'व्हल् अव्ह् अरा'उझल्) **उत्तेजनाची वाजवी पातळी :** state of moderate arousal.

oral stage - (ऑ'ऽरल् स्टेऽज्) **मौखिक अवस्था :** first stage in infant's life when it is mainly concerned with the pleasure received from mouth and its functions, according to Freud.

organising tendency - (ऑ'ऽगनाइझिंग टे'न्डन्सि) **संघटन प्रवृत्ती :** combining of innate physiological processes with experience to structure our perceptual field.

organizational psychology - (ऑ'ऽगनाइझेशनल साइकॉ'लजि) **संघटनात्मक मानसशास्त्र :** branch of industrial psychology dealing with structure and functions of an organization as related to problems.

orientation - (ऑ'ऽरिएन्टेऽशन्) **परिस्थितीचे भान :** awareness of situation and ability to use information appropriately.

orienting reaction - (ऑ'ऽरिअन्टिग् रिअं'क्शन्) **पवित्रा / रोख बदलणे** altering the stance to deal with new stimuli in its environment.

out groups - (आउट् ग्रूप्स) **बहिसमूह :** the group to which an individual: does not belong.

outcome measures - (आ'उट्कम् मे'झ्यऽ) **उपचार मूल्यमापन पद्धती :** ways of assessing the consequences of different forms of therapy.

outer directed - (आ'उटऽ डिरे'क्टेड्) **जनाभिमुखी :** exclusively confirming to social norms.

overachiever - (ओ'ऽव्हअची'व्हऽ) **अतिसंपादनशील :** a person who exceeds the level of achievement expected of him or her.

overcompensation - (ओ'ऽव्हकॉम्पेन्से'ऽशन्) **अतिप्रतिपूरण :** producing greater effort than is needed to overcome a defect or inferiority complex.

overconfirming - (ओ'ऽव्हऽकन्फ'ऽमिंग) **अतिअनुसरणशील :** being excessively slavish to the demands of authority or to conventions of social norms.

overies - (ओव्हरीज्) **डिंबग्रंथी :** female-sex-glands.

overlearning - (ओ'ऽव्हल'ऽनिंग) **अतिपठण/अतिअध्ययन :** learning in which practice or repetition continues beyond the point required for adequate mastery of the task.

overt - (ओ'ऽव्हऽट्) **उघड, व्यक्त :** open to public observation and not concealed.

■

P

pediatrics - (पी'डिॲट्रिक्स्) **बाल आरोग्य विज्ञान** : referring to childhood health and diseases.

paired associates technique - (पेऽअऽ असो'ऽशिअट् टेक्नी'क) **युग्म साहचर्य तंत्र** : learning technique where given first word of the pair of words, the participant is asked to recall the second.

paper and pencil test - (पे'ऽपऽ पे'न्स्ल् टेस्ट्) **कागद-पेन्सिल कसोटी** : a kind of test or projective technique which requires written answers.

paradoxical sleep - (पॅ'रडॉक्सिक्ल् स्लीप्) **विरोधाभासी निद्रा** : rem sleep of behavioural contradictions.

parakinesis - (पॅरअ्कि'नीऽसिस) **अतिमानसगती** : what appears to be movement of objects by unknown powers.

parallax - (पॅरलॅक्स्) **गतिमधील विरोध/सापेक्षगती** : the perception of objects as moving when the eyes are moved . Distant and near objects moving in opposite direction.

parallel distributed processing - (पॅ'रलेल् डिस्ट्रि'ब्यूटेड प्रसे'सिन्ग्) **समांतर माहिती संस्करण** : form of processing in which operations are distributed over a vast network and occur in parallel.

paranoia - (पॅ'रनॉ'इअ्) **संशय-विक्षोभ विकृती** : a psychosis characterised by delusions, especially dilusion of gandeur and delusion of persecution.

paranoid schizophrenia- (पॅ'रनॉ'इड् स्कि'ऽसोऽफ्री'न्यऽ) **संशय-विक्षोभ विमनस्कता** : a schizophrenic reaction in which the patient has delusion or persecution.

paranormal - (पॅ'रअ्नॉऽमल्) **पॅरासामान्य** : psychological events not explainable by scientific principles.

parapsychology - (पॅ'रऽसाइकॉ'लजि) **परामानसशास्त्र** : the branch of psychology dealing with paranormal phenomena observed by extra sensory perception.

parasympathetic branch : - (पॅ'रऽसि'म्पथे'टिक् ब्रँच) **परानुकंपी स्वायत्त नससंस्था** : the branch of autonomic nervous system monitoring relaxed state, and involved in conserving activity.

parathyroid glands - (पॅ'रऽथा'इअरॉइड् ग्लॅन्डस्) **उपकंठस्थ ग्रंथी** : endocrine glands situated near thyroid glands in the neck maintaining normal excitability of the nervous system.

parietal lobe - (पे'रिएटल् लोऽब्) **मध्यखंड** : portion of cerebral hemisphere, behind central fissuse and between the frontal and occipital lobes.

part methods - (पाऽट् मे'थडस्) **भाग पद्धती** : a technique of learning in which the material broken down in smaller parts is learned separately and then re-combined afterwards.

partial reinforcement - (पा'ऽशल् रीइन्फॉ'ऽस्मन्ट्) **सान्तर-प्रबलन/खंडित प्रबलन** : rewarding the organism intermittently for making correct response, rather than continuously.

participatory observation - (पाऽ'टिसिपेऽटरी ऑ'ब्झव्हे'ऽशन) **सहभागपूर्वक-निरीक्षण** : a research technique where an observer becomes an accepted member of group he or she wants to study.

patriarchy - (पे'ऽट्रिआऽकी) **पुरुषसत्ताक समाज** : a society run by men.

paternalism - (पॅ'टर्नॅलिझम्) **वडिलशाही** : withholding from adults power to make decisions about their own life.

peak experience - (पीक् इक्स्पि'अरिअन्स्) **(आत्मविष्काराची) अत्युच्च अनुभूती:** a moment of self-actualization according to humanistic psychology.

pecking order - (पे'किन्ग 'ऑऽड) **वर्चस्व श्रेणी** : dominance hierarchy.

peer group - (पिअऽ ग्रूप) **समवयस्कांचा समूह** : a social group with which one associates on more or less equal terms.

peer tutoring - (पिअऽ ट्युटॉ'ऽरिन्) **वडील भावंडांची शिकवणूक** : teaching of one child by another which is slightly older.

peg - board test - (पेग् बॉड्ड् टेस्ट्) **छिद्रयुक्त तक्ता-कसोटी** : performance test of manual dexterity in which pegs must be placed in holes as rapidly as possible.

peg - method - (पेग् मे'थड्) **खुंटी पद्धती** : items of information to be remembered are hanged on (peg) items which are well remembered.

penis envy - (पी'निस् ए'न्व्हि) **शिश्न ईर्षा** : refers to hypothesised envy of penis, universal among women, according to Freud, which leads to their castration complex.

penology - (पीनॉ्ऽलजि) **अपराधदंडनशास्त्र** : the study of criminal behaviour and its treatment.

perception - (पसे'प्शन्) **संवेदन** : the process of making sense out of the information received from the sense-organs.

perceptual defence - (प'ऽसेप्ट्युअल् डिफे'न्स्) **असुखद, अनिष्ट संवेदनापासून बचाव** : defending one's ego from the awareness of unpleasant perception by misperceiving or not perceiving them.

perceptual set / expectancy - (पसे'प्ट्युअल सेट / एक्स्पे'क्टन्सि) **सांवेदनिक न्यास / अपेक्षा** : the tendency / expectation to perceive stimuli in a particular way.

performance codes - (पर्फॉ'ऽमन्स् को'ऽड्स) **निर्वर्तनात्मक/कृती-संकेत** : the non - verbal communication codes in the form of eye contacts, facial expression, voice and gestures etc.

performance test - (पर्फॉ'ऽमन्स् टेस्ट्) **कृती कसोटी** : test where objects and non language means are used.

perceptual constancy - (पपे'चुअल् कॉ'न्स्टनसि) **संवेदनीय स्थिरता** : the tendency for perceived object to give rise to the same perceptual experiences in spite of wide variations in the conditions of observation.

peripheral nervous system - (परि'फरल् न'व्हस् सि'स्टम्) **(सीमावर्ती) परिसरीय नससंस्था** : part of nervous system that excludes brain and spinal cord, but consists of all other nerve cells in the body.

person perception - (प'ऽसन् पसे'प्शन) **व्यक्तीसापेक्ष संवेदन** : the process by which people form impression of others, then flesh them out and make them coherent.

persona - (पऽसो'ऽनऽ) **बाह्य व्यक्तिमत्त्व/मुखवटा** : the surface aspect of personality that people employ in their every-day social dealing.

personal space - (पऽसनल् स्पेऽस्) **व्यक्तिगत अवकाश** : area immediately surrounding the person is felt to be his own.

personality - (प'ऽसर्नॉलिटि) **व्यक्तिमत्त्व** : the semi-permanent internal predispositions that make people behave consistently, but in ways that differ from those of other people.

personality assessment - (प'सर्नॅ'लिटि असे'स्मन्ट्) **व्यक्तिमत्त्व मूल्यमापन:** the measurement or appraisal of personality.

personality inventory - (प'सर्नॅ'लिटि 'इनव्हन्ट्री) **व्यक्तित्त्व शोधिका** : an inventory for self appraisal, consisting of many statements about personal characteristics.

personality psychology - (प'सर्नॅ'लिटीऽ साइकॉ'लजी) **व्यक्तिमत्त्व मानसशास्त्र:** branch of psychology studying the differences between individuals and classifying them.

personality test - (प'सर्नॅ'लिटि टेस्ट्) **व्यक्तिमत्त्व कसोटी** : the test designed to assess personality characteristics of an individual.

personality trait - (प'सर्नॅ'लिटिऽ ट्रेऽट्) **व्यक्तिमत्त्व गुणघटक** : more or less enduring characteristics revealed in behaviour of a person.

personality type - (प'सर्नॅ'लिटिऽ टाइप) **व्यक्तिमत्त्व प्रकार** : any label used for classifying an individuals personality branch.

personnel psychology - (प'ऽस्ने'ल साइकॉ'लजी) **कर्मचारी मानसशास्त्र:** industrial psychology concerned with workers and job related factors.

Phallic stage - (फॅलिक स्टेज) **लिंगवर्ती अवस्था** : third stage of child is psychosexual life. According to Freud, when the child receives pleasure form his or her sex-organs and their functions.

phantasy - (फॅ'न्टझि) **दिवास्वप्न** : day-dreaming.

phenotype - (फेनो'टाइप) **(व्यक्तीच्या) वंशाणूची परिस्थिती प्रभावित वैशिष्ट्ये** : the observable characteristics of an individual, resulting from the interaction between genes and the environment.

phi-phenomenon - (फाय-फिनॉ'मिनन्) **फाय-प्रत्यय** : the impression of seeing apparent movement.

phobia - (फो'उबिअ) **भयगंड** : a morbid neurotic fear of a particular object or situation.

photographic memory - (फो'उटग्रॅ'फिक मे'मरी) **मूर्तिमंत/हुबेहुब स्मृती** : eidetic memory.

phrenology - (फ्रिना'लजि) **मस्तिष्कशास्त्र** : a pseudo science claiming that bumps on the surface of the skull are related to function.

physical self - (फि'झिकल् सेल्फ) **भौतिक-स्व** : the self which includes all physical objects belonging to the person.

physiognomy - (फि'झिऑ'नमि) **मुख-मुद्रा शास्त्र** : a pseudoscience attempting to define psychological characteristics from the structure of human face.

physiological motive - (फि'झिऑ'लजिकल् मो'उटिव्ह) **शारीरिक प्रेरक** : the motive that has some bodily basis.

physiological psychology - (फि'झिऑ'लजिकल् साइकॉ'लजि) **शरीर मानसशास्त्र** : the branch of psychology which studies the physiological processes underlying behaviour.

physiological reductionism - (फि'झिऑ'लजिकल् रिड'क्शनिझम्) **शरीरशास्त्रीय रूपांतरवाद** : explanations of complex behaviours in terms of simple physiological changes.

pictorial cues - (पिक्टॉ'उरिअल् क्यूज्) **चित्रातील (त्रिभिती) सूचके** : monocular cues to depth used by artists to create three dimensional impression.

pineal gland - (पिनियल ग्लॅन्ड्) **पिनियल ग्रंथी** : a very small endocrine gland located in the brain which produces melatonin and which is involved in circadian rhythm.

pitch - (पिच्) **स्वराची उच्चनीचता** : a qualitative dimension of hearing corrected with the frequency of sound waves.

pituitary gland - (पिट्युटरि ग्लॅन्ड्) **पीयुषिका** : an endocrine gland joined to the brain just below the hypothalamus regulating growth and other endocrine glands.

placebo effect - (प्लॅसी'बोउ इफेक्ट) **कृतक गुटी परिणाम** : a situation in which people experience some improvement from an empty, fake and ineffectual treatment.

play therapy - (प्लेइ थे'रपि) **क्रीडोपचार पद्धती** : a psychodynamic technique used for exploration of conflicts of children through symbolic play.

pleasure centre - (प्ले'झ्यइ से'न्टइ) **अधश्चेताक्षेपकातील सुखकेंद्र** : the area of hypothalamus which cause sensations of pleasure when electrically stimulated.

pleasure principle - (प्ले'झ्यइ प्रि'न्सिपल्) **सुखतत्त्व** : the drive to do things that produce pleasure or gratification.

pluralistic ignorance - (प्लु'अरॅ'लिस्टिक इ'ग्नरन्स्) **प्रत्येकाचे (सोयीस्कर) अज्ञान** : a situation in which individual believes himself to be the only exception to the accepted belief or behaviour of their group.

policy maker - (पॉ'लिसि मे'इकइ) **योजक/योजनातज्ज्ञ** : the expert who makes plans and guides the people after careful study of situation.

political leader - (पलि'टिकल ली'डइ) **राजकीय नेता** : the leader who seeks power and utilises power for political and social change.

polyandry - (पॉलिऑंड्रि) **बहुपतीत्व** : a mating system in which one female mates with many males.

population - (पॉ'प्युले'इशन) **लोकसमुदाय/उदाहरण-समुदाय** : the total universe of all possible cases from which the sample is selected.

positive concept of self - (पॉ'झिटिव्ह् कॉं'न्सेप्ट अव्ह सेल्फ्) **सकारात्मक स्व.** : one's belief that he/she is a good individual.

positive correlation - (पॉ'झिटिव्ह् कॉं'रिले'इशन) **धन-सहसंबंध** : two co-variables increasing at the same time.

positive incentive - (पॉ'झिटिव्ह् इन्से'न्टिव्ह्) **धन-प्रलोभन** : an object towards which behaviour is directed.

positive reinforcement - (पॉ'झिटिव्ह् रीइन्फॉ'इस्मन्ट्) **धन-प्रबलीकरण** : a way of increasing the strength of a given response by rewarding it, used in conditioning.

post conventional morality - (पोइस्ट् कन्व्हे'न्शनल मरॅ'लिटि) **विवेकनिष्ठनीतीः** self chosen consciously held system of rational ethical principles.

post partum depression - (पो'इस्ट् पा'ट्युऽडिप्रे'शन) **प्रसूतीनंतरची चेतापदशाः** depression following childbirth.

post-hypnotic suggestion - (पोऽस्ट् हिप्नॉ'टिक् सजे'स्चन्) **संमोहन पश्चात सूचना** : a suggestion made to a person under hypnosis which he or she carries out after coming out of the trance, without knowing the origin of suggestion.

pre- operational stage - (प्रीऑ'परे'ऽशनल् स्टेऽज्) **क्रियापूर्व (बोधात्मक) अवस्था** : coping with symbols but not with adult logic, according to Piget.

preconscious - (प्रीकॉ'न्शस्) **बोधपूर्व** : in psychoanalysis, something that is not present in consciousness at a given movement but which can be readily recalled.

pre-cognition - (प्री कॉ'ग्निशन्) **पूर्वज्ञान** : knowledge or cognition of a future event by extra-sensory perception.

preconventional morality - (प्रीकन्व्हे'न्शनल् मरॅ'लिटि) **विधिनिषेधाधारित नीती:** the morality characterised by pleasure principle and adults moral judgement.

prejudice - (प्रे'जडिस्) **पूर्वग्रह** : a negative, attitude with unverified belief towards members of same group.

presentation of self - (प्रेझन्टेऽशन् अव्ह् सेल्फ्) **स्व-सादरीकरण** : presenting oneself for favorable response of others.

pre-vision - (प्रीव्हि'इ्यन्) **भविष्यवेधी दृष्टी / पूर्वदृष्टी** : experience of seeing future events.

primacy effect - (प्रा'इमसि इफेक्ट) **प्राथम्य परिणाम/प्रारंभिक घटकांचा प्रभाव** : the high level recall of the first items in the list of first call.

primary abilities - (प्रा'इमरि अबि'लिटिज्) **प्राथमिक क्षमता** : the abilities, discovered by factor analysis, that underlie intelligence test - performance.

primary colours - (प्रा'इमरि कॅ'लऽ) **प्राथमिक / मूलभूत रंग** : the colours that are used in combination to produce any other view :blue, yellow, red, black and white.

primary group - (प्रा'इमरि ग्रूप) **प्राथमिक समूह** : a small group with direct and intimate personal relationships providing support and satisfaction or emotional needs to its members.

primary reinforcers - (प्रा'इमरि रीइन्फॉ'ऽसऽ) **प्राथमिक प्रबलके** : rewarding stimuli needed for living.

privation - (प्राइव्हे'ऽशन्) **संबंधाभाव / एकाकीपण** : lack of attachment.

pro-active interference - (प्रोॲक्टिव्ह् इ'न्ट'फि'अरन्स्) **भविष्यलक्षी निरोधन:** current learning being disrupted by previous learning.

probability - (प्रॉ'बबि'लिटि) **संभवनीयता** : the likelihood of occurrence of an event as against likelihood of alternative events.

problem solving skills - (प्रॉब्लम् सॉल्व्हिन्ग् स्किल्) **समस्या परिहारात्मक कौशल्ये** : ability to consider probable factors that influence outcome of each of various solutions to a problem.

procedural knowledge - (प्रसी'जऽल नॉ'लिज) **प्रत्यक्ष कृतीचे ज्ञान** : practical knowledge.

programmed learning - (प्रो'ऽगॅम्ऽ 'लऽनिन्ग) **क्रमबद्ध अध्ययन** : a form of learning in which tasks are broken down into individual frames and learning occurs step by step.

projection - (प्रजे'क्शन्) **प्रक्षेपण** : attributing one's feelings to other people unconsciously which are too threatening to one's ego.

projective technique - (प्रजे'क्टिव्ह् टेक्नी'क्) **प्रक्षेपण तंत्र** : procedures for uncovering a person's unconscious motivations, anxieties & conflicts.

proprioceptors - (प्रोप्रिओ'सेप्टअ(र)झ्) **स्थिती-गतीवेदनग्राहके** : sensory receptors that deal with information about the movement and orientation of the body.

pro-social behaviour - (प्रो-सोऽशल बिहे'ऽव्हयऽ) **समाजाभिमुख वर्तन** : behaviour which is beneficial to other.

pseudopsychology - (स्यू'डो साइकॉ'लजि) **मिथ्यामानसशास्त्र** : fake or false psychology.

psychasthenia - (सायकॅ'स्थेऽनीय) **मनोदुर्बलता** : weakness due to psychological disturbance.

psyche - (सा'इकि) **आत्मा/मन/स्व** : life force meaning soul mind or self.

psychic - (सा'इकिक) **अमानवी शक्तिधारी** : the person who is supposed to possess supernatural powers.

psychiatrist - (साइका'इअ'ट्रिस्ट्) **मनोविकृतीचिकित्सक** : a physician who specialises in psychiatry.

psychiatry : (साईका'इअट्रि) **मनोविकृतीशास्त्र** : the branch of medicine concerned with mental illness.

psychoanalyst - (सा'यकोऽऑनलिस्ट्) **मनोविश्लेषक** : apsycho-therapist who has been trained in the theory and technique of psychoanalysis.

psycho - sexual development - (सा'इकोसे'क्शुअल् डिव्हे'लप्मन्ट) **मनोलैंगिक विकास** : Freud's idea that development of child takes place through stages (oral, anal, phallic, latent and genital) culminating in adult sexuality.

psycho - social stages - (सा'इको-सोऽशल स्टेऽजिझ्) **मनोसामाजिक अवस्था:** modification of psycho-sexual development by adding some adult stages & emphasising social aspect.

psychoactive drug - (सा'इको'ऑक्टिव्ह ड्रग) **मन प्रभावकारी मादक द्रव्य** : any substance that alters mood, behaviour or conscious mental processes.

psychoanalysis - (सा'इकोऽअनॅ'लिसिस्) **मनोविश्लेषण** : Freud's set of theories about human behaviour and the form of treatment for mental disorders.

psychobiology - (सा'इकोबाइऑ'लजि) **मानस-जैवशास्त्र** : study of psychological process from a biological point of view.

psychodrama - (सा'इकोड्रा'ऽमऽ) **मनोनाट्य** : technique used in both diagnosis and psychotherapy where the patient is asked to act out certain things, in front of other patients and therapists.

psychogenic state - (सा'इकोजेनीक स्टेऽट) **मनोजन्य शरीरलक्षण** : a physical symptom, disease or emotional state which has mental origin.

psychokinesis - (सा'इकोकायनेसिस) **मन:प्रभावगती** : the ability to move objects and affect physical environment purely by power of mind - a parapsychological supposition.

psycholinguistics - (सा'इकोलिं'ग्वि'स्टिक्स्) **मानसभाषा विज्ञान** : the study of relationship between the nature, structure and use of language and the psychological processes of the user.

psychological altruism - (साइ'कलॉ'जिक्ल् अॅ'लट्रुइझम्) **मानसशास्त्रीय परहितवाद** : altruistic behaviour arising from cognitive rather than biological processes.

psychological dependence - (साइ'क्लॉं'जिक्ल् डिपे'न्डन्स्) **मानसिक अवलंबन** : habitual use of drug to relieve anxiety even though no physical dependence had developed.

psychological motive - (साइ'क्लॉं'जिक्ल् मो'उटिव्ह्) **मानसिक प्रेरक** : a motive that is primarily learned rather than based on biological needs.

psychological self - (साइ'क्लॉं'जिक्ल् सेल्फ्) **मानसिक 'स्व'** : all mental abilities and characteristic a person belongs.

psychological warfare - (साइ'क्लॉं'जिक्ल् वॉं'उफेऽअ) **मानसशास्त्रीय युद्ध:** application of psychological research to the manipulation of attitudes in warfare to lower the enemy's morale.

psychologism - (साइकॉं'लजिझम्) **मानसशास्त्र प्राथम्यवाद** : the view that all questions about human beings are reducible to psychology.

psychologist's fallacy - (साइकॉं'लजिस्ट फॅं'लसि) **मानसशास्त्रज्ञाचा विचारदोष:** a fallacy where a psychologist reads into someone else's mind what is present in his own.

psychology - (साइकॉं'लजि) **मानसशास्त्र** : the scientific study of mental processes & behaviour.

psychometry - (साइकॉं'मेट्री) **मनोमापनशास्त्र** : refers to tests and measures of psychological factors including intelligence tests.

psychomotor - (सायको'मो'उटऽ) **मनोकारक** : refers to effects of mental processes on the actions of muscles.

psychopath - (सा'इकोऽपॅथ्) **मनोविकृत** : the anti-social personality characterised by lack of conscience.

psychopharmacology - (सायको'उफाऽमकॉलजीऽ) **मानसऔषधीशास्त्र** : the study of effects of drugs on psychological functioning.

psychophysical methods - (सायको'फिजिकल मेथड्स) **मानसभौतिकीय पद्धती:** procedures used to determine thresholds of sensory modalities.

psychophysics - (सायको'फिजिक्स) **मानसभौतिकी** : the study of relationship between physical stimuli and subjective sensations they produce.

psychosis - (सा'इकोऽसिस) **मनोविकृती** : a psychological disorder, characterised by a lack of contact with reality, requiring institutional treatment.

psychosomatic - (साइको'समॅ'टिक्) **मनोकायिक** : relating to psychological disorders in which emotional stress produces physiological symptoms.

psychosurgery - (साइकोस'उजरि) **मानसशस्त्रक्रिया** : surgery in which sections of brain are removed or lesions are made to treat a psychological conditions.

psychotherapy - (साइको'थे'रपि) **मानसोपचार पद्धती** : the use of psychological techniques to treat psychological disturbances.

psychotic behaviour - (सा'इकोटिक् बिहे'उव्हऽ) **मनोविकृत/दुर्मनस्क वर्तन:** behaviour indicating gross impairment in reality contact.

pubescence - (प्यू'बसन्स) **पौगंडावस्था** : the stage of attaining puberty.

public - opinion - (पॅ'ब्लिक् अपि'न्यन्) **लोकमत** : the opinion expressed by the public about a particular problem.

punishment - (प'निश्मन्ट्) **शिक्षा/दंड** : a procedure used to decrease the strength of a response by presenting an aversive stimulus.

pure self - (प्यूअसेल्फ़्) **शुद्ध स्व:** the highest spiritual knowledge about oneself.

purposive group - (प'उपसिव्ह् ग्रूप्) **सहेतुक समूह** : the group acting for the fulfillment of a definite purpose.

pyknic type - ('पिकनिक टाऽइप) **स्थूल/मेदप्रधान** : the person with fat body.

■

Q-sort - (क्यू सॉर्ट्) **क्यू निवडतंत्र / एक व्यक्तिमत्व गुणघटक निर्धारण तंत्र:** a technique for rating personality traits.

quasi experimental research - (क्वे'ऽसाइ इक्स'पेरिमन्ट रि'सऽच) **तत्सम प्रायोगिक संशोधन पद्धती :** research similar to experiment but lacking in direct manipulation of independent variable.

quasi group - (क्वे'ऽसाइ ग्रूप) **तत्सम समूह :** an aggregate of persons, which is yet to form a true group.

questionnaire survey - (क्वे'स्टिऑने'अ स'ऽव्हेऽ) **प्रश्नावली सर्वेक्षण :** a survey requiring written answer to questions.

quiet sleep - (क्वा'इअट् स्लीप्) **स्थिर नेत्र निद्रा :** non - rapid eye movement sleep.

quota sampling - (क्वोऽटऽ सा'ऽम्पलिंग) **नियतांश नमुनाचयन :** sampling data from each subgroup of a given population.

■

R

radical behaviourism - (रॅ'डिकल बिहे'ऽव्हऽरिझम्) **कट्टर वर्तनवाद :** the view that all behaviour is learned.

random - (रॅ'न्डम्) **आकस्मिक :** occurring without voluntary control, occuring by chance.

random sampling - (रॅन्डम् सा'म्पलिंग) **आकस्मिक-नमुना निवड :** selecting participants on random basis so that every member of population has equal chance to be selected.

randomisation - (रॅ'न्डमायझेशन) **अनियतीकरण :** the process of random selection.

random selection - (रॅ'न्डम् सिले'क्शन्) **अनियत निवड :** accidental selection, selection without applying any specific rules of selection.

rapport - (रॅपाँ's) **मनोमिलाप/सुसंवाद :** a comfortable relationship between subject and tester.

rating scale - (रेऽटिंग स्केऽल्) **पदनिश्चय श्रेणी :** graded scale for measurement and assessment of a characteristic.

rational emotive therapy - (रॅ'शनल इमो'ऽटिव्ह् थे'रपि) **विकासाधारित भावनिक-चिकित्सा :** a form or cognitive therapy which aims to produce rational thinking by challenging irrational beliefs.

rationalisation - (रॅ'शनलायझेशन) **मिथ्या समर्थन/वृथासमर्थन :** a defence mechanical where a person justifies behaviour by giving socially approvable reasons to protect his ego.

reaction - time - (रिअॅ'क्शन टाईम्) **प्रतिक्रिया काल :** the time elapsed between presentation of a stimulus and the participant's response to it.

reaction formation - (रिॲ'क्शन फॉ'ऽमे'ऽशन) **प्रतिक्रिया घडण :** defence mechanism where a person deals with unconscious threatening drives by reacting consciously in the opposite direction.

reactive depression - (री'ॲक्टिव्ह डिप्रे'शन) **बाह्यकारणोभ्दव चेतापदशा** depression resulting from external causes.

reality principle - (रिॲ'लिटी प्रि'न्सिपुल्) **वास्तव तत्त्व :** Freud's explanation for motivating force of the ego, which accommodates the demands of the environment in realistic way.

recall - (रिकॉ'ऽल) **प्रत्यावाहन :** retrieving and being able to reproduce information from memory.

recency effect - (री'सन्सी इफे'क्ट्) **निकटपूर्णवर्तित्त्वाचा परिणाम :** good free recall of the last few items in the list based on information in the short term memory.

receptor - (रिसे'प्टर) **ग्राहक नसपेशी :** a sensory nerve ending which responds to a particular kind of stimulus.

recessive gene - (रिसि'सिव्ह जीन) **अप्रभावी जनुक :** a gene that remains latent because it is paired with a dominant gene.

reciprocal altruism - (रिसि'प्रक्ल् ॲ'ल्टुइझम) **विलंबित प्रति-परोपकार अपेक्षा :** a selfless act anticipating similar act at a later date.

reciprocal punishment - (रिसि'प्रक्ल प'निश्मन्ट्) **शिक्षेची अनुरूपता :** the view that the form of punishment should fit the crime.

recitation - (रे'सिटेऽशन्) **मौखिक प्रत्यावाहन :** repeating orally whatever is learned earlier.

recognition - (रे'कग्नि'शन) **प्रत्यभिज्ञा :** identifying information previously experienced and stored in memory.

reconstructive memory - (री'कन्स्ट्रॅ'क्टिव्ह मे'मरि) **पुनर्रचित स्मृती :** the form of memory recall not an accurate reproduction of original stimulus, but is distorted by schemas that have filled in the gaps.

recovered memory - (री'कं'व्हऽ मे'मरि) **दमित अनुभवांचे स्मरण :** memory brought into conscious experience which was repressed through hypnosis or psychotherapy.

reference group - (रे'फरन्स् ग्रुप्) **संदर्भ-समूह :** a group with which a person identifies and follows group-norms, though he is not a member or yet to get membership of that group.

reflex - (री'फ्लेक्स्) **प्रतिक्षेप** : the innate and automatic response to a stimulus.

reformative theory of punishment - (रिफॉ'र्मटिव्ह् थिअरि अव्ह् प'निश्मन्ट्) **शिक्षेची सुधारणावादी उपपत्ती** : the theory of punishment aiming at improvement in behaviour of the criminal.

reformer - (रिफॉ'र्मऽ) **सुधारणावादी नेता** : a typical leader who attempts to bring out social changes through the process of enlightenment.

refractory phase - (रिफ्रॅ'क्टरि फेज़्) **अक्षमतेचा काल** : the period of inactivity in neuron after it has fired once.

regression - (रिग्रे'शन्) **परागमन** : returning to earlier stages of development when under severs stress.

rehearsal - (रिह'ऽस्ल्) **उजळणी** : the verbal repetition of given information, which strengthens its memory trace.

reinforcement - (रीइन्फॉ'ऽस्मन्ट्) **प्रबलीकरण** : refers to the behaviour likely to re-occur because the response is agreeable

retributive theory of punishment - (रेट्रिब्युटिव्ह् थिअरि अव्ह् प'निश्मन्ट्) **शिक्षेची प्रतिशोध उपपत्ती** : the theory of punishment which states that punishment serves the purpose of getting satisfaction through revenge.

relative morality - (रेलटिव्ह् मरॅ'लिटि) **साध्य सापेक्ष नीती** : morality based on the notion that ends can justify means.

relaxation - (री'लॅक्से ऽशन) **शिथिलावस्था** : state of low tension, where emotional level is diminished.

reliability - (रि'लाइअबि'लिटी) **विश्वसनीयता** : the extent to which the research study produces consistent findings over time.

rem sleep - (रेम स्लीप) **जलद नेत्र-हालचालीची निद्रा/स्वप्ननिद्रा** : rapid eye movement sleep .

repeated measures design - (रिपी'टेड मे'झ्यस डिझा'इन्) **प्रयुक्त पुनरावर्तन आराखडा** : a research design where the same participants are used for all conditions in the experiment.

repetition compulsion - (रे'पिटि'शन् कम्प'ल्शन्) **सक्तीची पुनरावृत्ती** : a complusion to repeat the same behaviour over and over again.

replicability - (रे'प्लिकबिलिटि) **पुनरावर्तनीयता** : research in which findings of an experiment can be repeated.

representative heuristics - (रेप्रिझे'न्टटिव्ह ह्युअरि'स्टिक) **प्रातिनिधिक नवगामी:** 'rule of thumb' which enable judgement to be made on the basis of probability.

representative sample - (रेप्रिझे'न्टटिव्ह सा'म्पल) **प्रातिनिधिक नमूना :** a sample that is intended to be completely representative of the population from which it is drawn.

repression - (रिप्रे'शन) **दमन :** a defence mechanism where by memories causing anxiety are kept out of conscious awareness to protect the individual.

Rosenthal effect - (रोझेन्थल इफे'क्ट्) **रोझेन्थल परिणाम :** a form of experimental bias or self-fulfilling profecy in social setting suggested by Robert Rosenthal

response - (रिस्पॉ'न्स्) **प्रतिक्रिया :** the behavioral result of stimulation in form of a movement.

response bias - (रिस्पॉ'न्स् बा'इअस्) **प्रतिसादाची विशिष्ट तऱ्हा :** the mental set to respond in a particular way to issues or questions.

resting potential - (रेस्टिंग पोऽटेन्शल) **क्रियाविभव :** the exchange of inside and outside ions of the neurons.

reticular formation - (रिटि'क्युलर फॉर्मे'ऽशन) **जालमय उद्दिपक यंत्रणा :** nerve paths within brain stem, lying outside well-defined pathways, and important as an arousal mechanism.

retrival - (रिट्री'व्हल्) **आठवणे :** recovering stored information and remembering it.

retro - active interference - (रे'ट्रोऽ-ऑक्टिव्ह इ'न्टफि'अरन्स्) **भूतलक्षी निरोधन :** subsequent learning disrupting memory of previous learning.

retrograde amnesia - (रे'ट्रोग्रेड् ऑम्नी'शिअ) **अपघातजनक प्रसंगापूर्वींचे विस्मरण :** the inability to recall the events leading up to the trauma that induced amnesia.

reward - (रीवार्ड) **पारितोषिक :** positive reinforcement.

right to withdraw - (राइट् टू विड्ड्रॉ'ऽ) **सहभाग निवृत्तीचा हक्क :** basic right of the participant in research study to stop his involvement at any point.

rods - (रॉड्स) **दंडपेशी :** photoreceptors in the retina specialised for vision in dim light and for detection of movement.

role - (रोऽल) **भूमिका :** the kind of behaviour expected of a given person in a given situation.

role-playing - (रोऽल प्ले'ऽइन्ग्) **भूमिका वठवणे :** acting the part of another person in a therapeutic or experimental situation.

Romeo and Juliet effect - (रोमिओ ॲन्ड् ज्युलिएट इफे'क्ट) **पालक विरोधातून प्रणयपुष्टी :** an experimental finding that parental opposition can lead to the strengthening of a young couple's love.

Rorschach test - (रोर्शा टेस्ट) **रोर्शा कसोटी :** famous projective technique consisting of ten standardised inkblots.

rote learning - (रोऽट् ल'ऽर्निंग्) **घोकंपट्टी :** learning solely through repetitions without any attempt to find meaning or order in the materials.

saccadic movement - (सॅकॅडिक् मूव्ह्मन्ट्) **नजर फिरणे नेत्रप्लुती :** jumping of the eyes from one point of fixation to another.

sadism - (सॅडिझम) **परपीडनरती :** sexual pleasure desired through inflicting physical pain.

sado- masochism - (सॅडो-मॅ'सकिझ्म्) **परपीडन-आत्मपीडनरती :** the tendency towards both sadism and masochism.

same-side transfer - (सेम साइड ट्रॉन्स्फ़5) **पक्ष संक्रमण :** transfer of learning from any side of the body to its same-side.

sample - (सा'स्म्पल्) **नमूना :** a group of cases studied as representatives of the population from which they are drawn.

satyriasis - (सॅटि'रिऑसिस्) **पुरुष-कामोन्माद :** an obsession with sex in men.

scapegoat - (स्के'ऽप्गोऽट्) **बळीचा बकरा/अजापुत्रबळी :** the object of displaced aggression, that is victimied.

schemas - (स्कीमाज्) **आकृतीबंध :** organised pkackets of information stored in the long term memory.

schizoid- (स्कि'ऽसोइड) **खिन्नमनस्कतासंबंधित :** relating to schizophrenia.

schizophrenia - (स्कि'ऽसोऽफ्री'न्यऽ) **छिन्नमनस्कता :** a severe disorder in which there is a loss of contact with reality, including distortions of thought, emotion and behaviour.

scholastic test - (स्कलॅ'स्टिक् टेस्ट) **शालेय कसोटी :** any test in the school subject.

school psychologist - (स्कूल साइकॉ'लजिस्ट्) **शालेय मानसशास्त्रज्ञ** : a professional psychologist employed by a school with responsibility to solve educational problem at school level.

Seashore test - (सीशोअर टेस्ट) **सांगितिक कसोटी** : a series of recorded tests of musical abilities developed by Carl Seashore.

secondary motives - (से'कन्डरि मो'उटिव्ह्स) **दुय्यम प्रेरके** : learned motives which are universal in culture and for which the bodily basis is not known.

secondary reinforcer - (से'कन्डरि री'इन्फॉ'उसस) **दुय्यम प्रबलक** : a stimulus which is rewarding as it has been associated with primary reinforcer.

secondary sex characteristics - (से'कन्डरि सेक्स् कॅ'रक्टरि'स्टिक्स्) **दुय्यम लिंगसंलग्न वैशिष्ट्ये** : the physical features distinguishing the mature male from mature female, apart from reproductive organs.

sedatives - (से'डटिव्ह्) **प्रशांतके** : substances or drugs which release tension.

selective attention - (सिले'क्टिव्ह् अटे'न्शन्) **निवडपूर्वक अवधान** : the deliberate focusing of attention on something to the exclusion of competing stimuli.

self - denial - (सेल्फ् डिना'इअल्) **स्व-इच्छांना नकार** : an act or practice of forgoing satisfaction of desires.

self - efficacy - (सेल्फ् ए'फिकसि) **स्व-नैपुण्य/स्व-सामर्थ्य** : an individual's assessment of his or her ability to cope with given situations.

self - esteem - (सेल्फ् इस्टी'म्) **स्व-आदर** : it refers to how well a person likes himself, how worthy he or she seems himself or herself to be.

self - evaluation - (सेल्फ् इव्हॅ'ल्युए'उशन्) **स्वमूल्यमापन** : rating or judgement made by the individual about himself.

self - handicapping - (सेल्फ् हॅ'न्डिकॅपिंग्) **आत्मघातकी कृती** : actions that people take to subotage their performance.

self - (सेल्फ्) **'स्व'** : part of personality that is conscious of its identity over time.

self- actualisation need - (सेल्फ् ॲ'क्युअलायझेशन नीड्) **आत्मविष्करण** : the need to discover and fulfil one's potential.

self- fulfilling proficiency - (सेल्फ् फुल्फि'लिंग प्रफि'शन्सि) **अपेक्षेतून अपेक्षापूर्तींचे पूर्वकथन :** the idea that expectations about something lead to expected behaviour in future.

self regulation - (सेल्फ् रे'ग्युले'उशन्) **(कृतीच्या आतरिक मानकाचे) स्वनियंत्रण:** a process of self regard if an internal standard of performance is achieved but feelings of failure if it is not achieved.

self-concept - (सेल्फ् कॉ'न्सेप्ट्) **स्व-संकल्पना :** all the elements which make up a person's view of himself or herself, including self - image.

self-discovery - (सेल्फ् डिस्कि'व्हरि) : approach to learning in which child is encouraged to use its initiative in learning.

self-identity - (सेल्फ आइडे'न्टिटि) **स्व-तादात्म्यभाव :** knowing, recognising and trying to be true to one's abilities and characteristics.

self-image - (सेल्फ इ'मिज्) **स्व-प्रतिमा :** the self which a person believes himself or herself to be.

self-serving bias - (सेल्फ-स'उव्हिन्ग् बा'इयस्) **स्व-अनुकूलता पूर्वग्रह :** the tendency to take credit for one's success, but not to accept blame for one's failures.

semantic coding - (सिमॅ'न्टिक् कोडिंग) **अर्थपर विसंकेतन :** encoding or processing words in terms of their meaning based on information stored in long-term memory.

semantic memory - (सिमॅ'न्टिक् मे'मरी) **अर्थपर स्मृती :** organised knowledge about the world and about language stored in long-term memory.

semicircular canals - (से'मिस'उक्युलउ कनॅ'ल्स्) **अर्धवर्तुळाकार कडी :** three fluid filled canals located in inner ear passing information about movement and balance to the brain.

senescence - (सेने'सन्स) **वार्धक्य/वृद्धावस्था :** psychological stresses and conflicts of old age & ageing process as well as unique & positive aspects of old-age.

senile dementia - (सी'नाइल् डिमे'न्सिआ) **वार्धक्य अवमनस्कता :** a degenerative condition found in old people which includes later stages of Alzheimer's disease.

sensation - (सेन्से'उशन्) **वेदन :** the experience following the stimulation of a sense organ and a necessary pre- requisite of preception.

sensitisation - (से'न्सिटाइझ़ेशन्) **वेदनशीलता अध्ययन** : a form of learning in which an organism learns to strengthen its reaction to a weak stimulus if a threatening or painful stimulus follows.

sensitivity training - (से'न्सिटि'व्हिटि ट्रे॒निंग्) **संवेदन क्षमता प्रशिक्षण** : a technique used for improving interpersonal communication and relationships.

sensory adaptation - (से'न्सरि अडॅ'प्शन) **वेदनिक प्रतियोजन** : neglect of sensation by the receptors themselves.

sensory buffer - (से'न्सरि बं'फ5) **संवेदनप्रक्रियेतील संस्करणाचा प्रारंभिक टप्पा** : an early part of the processing system, in which information stays for a short period of time before being attended to or disappearing from the system.

sensory deprivation - (से'न्सरि डे'प्रिव्हे'ऽशन्) **वेदनिक वंचितता** : a situation where people are deprived of the usual stimulation of their senses.

sensory memory - (से'न्सरि मे'मरि) **वेदनिक स्मृती** : the first stage of memory - process, lasting less than a second during which information is recorded by the sense organs.

sentiment - (से'न्टिमन्टस्) **स्थायीभाव** : relatively permanent mood.

scoffolding - (स्कॅफोल्डिंग) **बालकांच्या बोधात्मक कौशल्यास वाव देणे** : providing opportunities to children for development of cognitive skills.

separation - (से'परे'ऽशन) **दुरावा** : absence of the caregiver.

separation anxiety - (से'परे'ऽशन् अॅन्झा'इअटि) **दुरावाजन्य, चिंताव्याकुलता:** the sense of anxiety felt by a child when separated from their attachment figure.

separation protest - (से'परे'ऽशन् प्रटे'स्ट्) **दुराव्यास विरोध** : infants behaviour when separated, crying out or holding out their arms.

serial learning - (सि'अरिअल् ल'ऽनिंग्) **क्रमवार अध्ययन** : learning the material in a particular order or sequence.

serial reproduction - (सि'अरिअल् रीप्रडं'क्शन्) **माहितीचे क्रमाक्रमाने परिवर्तन:** changing of information as it passes between different people.

serotonin - (सेरॉटॉनिन) **सेरोटॉनिन** : a neuro transmitter that is associated with lower arousal, sleepiness and reduced anxiety.

servomechanism - (स'ऽव्हीमे'कनिझ़म्) **प्रणाली नियंत्रक प्रणाली** : a system that controls another system.

sex - (सेक्स्) **लिंग** : the biological fact of being male or female as determined by a pair or chromosomes.

sex-chromosome - (सेक्स-क्रोमोसोम) **लिंगसंलग्र रंगसूत्र** : X or Y chromosome which determines the sex of the individual.

sex-education - (सेक्स् एʼड्युकेʼऽशन्) **लैंगिक शिक्षण** : instructing in physiological reproduction and in attitudes promoting good sexual adjustment towards sexuality in general & marriage in particular.

shame culture - (शेऽम् केंʼल्चऽ) **लज्जा संस्कृती** : the culture that relies on shaming and ridiculing by others to regulate the behaviour for maintaining social control.

shape constancy - (शेऽप्-कॉʼन्स्टन्सि) **रूपसातत्य /आकारसातत्य** : the tendency to see a familiar object as of the same shape regardless of the viewing angle.

shaping - (शेऽपिंग) **आकारण** : the process by which persuit of small, intermediate goals leads to the achievement of final goal.

short-term memory - (शॉऽट् टऽम् मेʼमरि) **अल्पकालिक स्मृती** : a temporary place for storing data where they receive minimal processing and are shortlived unless maintained through rehearsals.

sibling - (सिʼबलिन्ग्) **बंधुभावी व्यक्ती/बहिण भाऊ** : a brother or a sister.

sibling rivalry - (सिʼबलिन्ग् राʼइव्हलि) **भावंडांमधील मत्सर** : competition between children in family usually for the affection of parents

single blind study - (सिंगल ब्लाईंड स्टडी) **एकांध अभ्यास** : experimental design where the patients under investigation do not know the treatment and non-treatment conditions during the experiment.

signal detection theory - (सिग्रल् डिटेʼक्शन् थिʼअरि) **संकेत शोधन उपपत्ती:** perception of a stimulus is related to the sensitivity of the sense receptors and the motivation of the individual to respond.

significant other - (सिग्रिʼफिकन्ट् अॅʼदऽ) **(स्वप्रतिमासंदर्भातील) अन्य महत्वपूर्ण व्यक्ती** : the person who is particularly important to us in relation to our self image.

simulation - (सʼम्युलेऽशन्) **प्रतिरूपण** : a training technique applied in industry where original machine-like structures, the simulators are used.

situational attributions - (सि'ट्युएऽशन्ल् ॲट्रिब्यु'शन्) **परिस्थितीवरील गुणारोपण** : people's actions are supposed to be caused by situations they experience and not by their personalities.

size constancy - (साइझ् कॉ'न्स्टन्सि) **आकारमानसातत्य** : the tendency to see a familiar object as of its actual size regardless of its distance.

Skinner box - (स्किनर बॉक्स्) **स्किनर कूटपेटी** : boxlike structure used to demonstrate trials & error learning in which the correct operation of mechanism, brings the animal a reward.

sleep centre - (स्लीप् से'न्ट्ऽ) **अधश्श्रेतक्षेपकातील निद्राकेन्द्र** : an area of hypothalamus that induces sleep when electrically stimulated or removed by surgery.

sleep talking - (स्लीप् टॉ'किंग्) **झोपेत बरळणे** : speaking words or sentences in deep-sleep which are unclear and difficult to make sense.

sleeper effect - (स्ली'पऽ इफे'क्ट्) **संशोधनोत्तर अभिवृत्ती परिवर्तन** : change in an attitude or opinion after a study has been conducted.

sleep-walking - (स्लीप् वॉ'ऽकिन्ग्) **निद्रा भ्रमण** : walking about in the state of sleep, not moving consciously, being somewhat suggestible and likely to commit accident.

slip of tongue - (स्लिप् अव्ह टंग्) **वाचेची गफलत/तोंडातून निसटलेले शब्द** : occasionally uttered words or sentences by the subject that underlie unconscious desires or impulses.

social attitude - (सो'ऽशल् ॲटिट्यूड) **सामाजिक अभिवृत्ती** : a predisposition to behave in a particular way towards people which has cognitive, emotive & behavioural dimensions.

social causation hypothesis - (सो'ऽशल् कॉ'झेशन हाइपॉ'थिसिस्) **सामाजिक कारणविषयक अभ्युपगम** : the hypothesis that schizophrenia is related to greater stress experienced by lower class as compared to middle class.

social cognition - (सो'ऽशल् कॉ'ग्निशन) **सामाजिक बोधन** : the information processing of our social environment including our attribution of social behaviour.

social cohesion - (सो'ऽशल् कोऽही'इ्यन्) **समूहऐक्य :** the attraction that a group has for its members that helps to bind it together.

social Darwinism - (सो'ऽशल् डार्विनिझम्) **सामाजिक डार्विनवाद :** application of Darwin's evolutionary theory of natural selection to human society.

social deprivation - (सो'ऽशल् डे'प्रिव्हे'ऽशन) **सामाजिक वंचितता :** the situation where an individual or a group does not have the benefits common to a given society.

social development - (सो'ऽशल् डिव्हे'लप्मन्ट) **सामाजिक विकसन :** the development of the individual's social competence including social skills and ability to build social relationships

social distance scale - (सो'ऽशल् डि'स्टन्स स्केल) **सामाजिक अंतर(मापक) श्रेणी :** the scale devised to measure the degree of social intimacy of a person to other person or group.

social drift hypothesis - (सो'ऽशल् ड्रिफ्ट् हाइपॉ'थिसिस्) **सामाजिक स्थानांतर अभ्युपगम :** the hypothesis that schizophrenia is caused because poorer number drift into that group due to their inability to cope.

social facilitation - (सो'ऽशल् फसि'लिटेऽशन) **सामाजिक सौकर्य :** the enhancement of individual's performance when working in the presence of other people.

social influence - (सो'ऽशल् इ'न्म्लुअन्स) **सामाजिक प्रभाव :** the influence of a group or individual on thinking attitudes and behaviour of others.

social interaction - (सो'ऽशल् इ'न्टरॅ'क्शन्) **सामाजिक आंतरक्रिया :** the mutual influence that people have on each others behaviour in a social setting.

social learning theory - (सो'ऽशल् ल'ऽनिंग थि'अरी) **सामाजिक अध्ययन उपपत्ती :** the view that behaviour can be explained in terms of both direct and indirect reinforcement.

social loafing - (सो'ऽशल् लॉ'फिंग) **सामाजिक कामचुकारपणा :** tendency to work less as part of a group than as individual due to diffusion of responsibility.

social norms - (सो'ऽशल् नॉऽम्स्) **सामाजिक मानदंड :** the standards of rules or behaviour for individuals expected by a given society or culture.

social penetration theory - (सो'ऽश्ल् पे'निट्रेऽशन् थि'अरि) **सामाजिक घनिष्ठता समरसता उपपत्ती** : the theory that the development of a relationship involves increasing self disclosure on both side.

social perception - (सो'ऽश्ल् पसे'पशन) **सामाजिक संवेदन** : this refers to how we use our data from our environment to perceive our social world.

social psychology - (सो'ऽश्ल् साइकॉ'लजि) **सामाजिक मानसशास्त्र** : the branch of psychology which deals with behaviour of individuals and people in social situations.

social status - (सो'ऽश्ल् स्टे'ऽट्स्) **सामाजिक दर्जा** : position in society, in relation to and as determined by other people.

socialisation - (सो'ऽशलायझेशन्) **सामाजिकीकरण** : the process whereby an individual becomes a social being.

socio emotional leader - (सो'सिऑ इमो'ऽशनल् ली'डऽ) **समाज भावनावेधी नेता** : a person who keeps up the morale and facilities the interpersonal relationship of the group.

sociolinguistics - (सो'सिऑलिं'ग्वि'स्टिक्स्) **सामाजिक भाषाविज्ञान** : scientists who argue that language functions in social context and it is important to study it in this context.

sociometry - (सो'ऽसिऑमेट्री) **समाजमिती तंत्र** : the technique for measurement of social relationship and social attraction.

somatic nervous system - (सोमॅटिक नर्व्हस सिस्टिम) **कायिक नससंस्था** : the branch of the peripheral nervous system consisting of nerves that connect the brain and spinal cord with the sense receptors, muscles and body surface.

somatic therapy - (सोमॅटिक थे'रपी) **कायिक उपचार पद्धती** : a form of treatment or mental illness involving manipulation of the body.

somatotonia - (सोमॅटोटोनिया) **देहबल्यता/उत्साहशीलता** : the characteristic of a person with sound constitution of body.

source trait - (सॉऽस् ट्रेऽ) **मूळ गुणघटक** : a hypothetical 'deep' trait accounting for the surface traits.

sour - grapes reaction - (साउअ-ग्रेप्स रीअँ'क्शन्) **आंबट-द्राक्षे प्रतिक्रिया** : convincing oneself that something one cannot have is not worth having any way (A form of rationalisation)

space -error - (स्पेस् ए'रऽ) **स्थल प्रमाद :** error arising in same experiments due to relative positions of two stimuli.

spaced practice - (स्पेऽस्ड् प्रॅं'क्टिस्) **खंडित सराव :** any learning with a time interval between practices.

spatial memory - (स्पेऽशल् मे'मरि) **अवकाशिक स्मृती :** memory for the layout of one's environment.

spatio- temporal codes - (स्पॅशिओ टेंपरल कोड) **स्थल-कालात्मक संकेत :** codes about non-verbal communication related to spatial and temporal events.

speech accomodation - वाचिक संयोजन : the theory that people modify the way they speak to suit the context.

speech therapy - (स्पीच् थे'रपि) **वाचोपचार :** a therapy that is directed to the correction of speech disorder.

spindle sleep - (स्पिंडल स्लीप) **गुंगीची झोप :** the stage two sleep consisting of short bursts of rhythmical responses of 13 to 16 Hz slightly higher than alpha.

split personality - (स्प्लिट् प'ऽसनॅं'लिटी) **दुभंग व्यक्तिमत्व :** a set of psychological processes split off from rest of individual's personality.

split-brain technique - (स्प्लिट्-ब्रेऽन् टेक्नी'क्) **मेंदू-विभक्तीकरण तंत्र :** separating the brain at corpus callosum so as to study different functions of the brain.

spontaneous recovery - (स्पॉन्टे'ऽन्यस् रिकॅ'व्हरि) **उत्स्फूर्त पुनर्स्थापन :** the reemergence of responses over time following experimental extinction.

sports psychology - (स्पॉऽट्स् सायकॉ'लजि) **क्रीडा-मानसशास्त्र :** the study of human behaviour in sports.

SQ3R- method - (एस क्यू श्री आर मेथड) **एस्क्यू श्री आर पद्धती :** study methods to aid textbook learning consisting of five steps namely surveying, questioning, reading, reciting and reviewing.

stage theory - (स्टेऽज् थि'अरि) **क्रमबद्ध विकासाची उपपत्ती :** a theory which conceives developmental process taking place is sequential, progressive steps according to Piget.

standard deviation - (स्टॅं'न्डड्ड् डी'व्हिए'शन) **प्रमाण विचलन :** the measure of spread of scores around the mean.

standardised tests - (स्टॅ'न्डडाइझ्ड टेस्ट्) **प्रमाणित कसोट्या** : tests that have been used with large groups of individuals in order to establish 'standards' or 'norms'.

Stanford -Binet test - (स्टॅनफोर्ड बिने टेस्ट) **बुद्धिमापन कसोटी** : an individual's intelligence test, revision of Binet-scale, originally done at Stanford University in 1916.

state dependent learning - (स्टेइट् डिपे'न्डन्ट् ल'ऽर्निंग) **अवस्था-अवलंबी अध्ययन** : the form of learning in which a person relies on a match between his emotional or physical state at the time of an event and at the time of retrieval as a cue to recall.

statistical significance - (स्टटि'स्टिक्ल् सिग्नि'फिकन्स्) **संख्याशास्त्रीय लक्षणीयता** : the level at which the decision is made to reject null hypothesis. in favour of experimental hypothesis.

stereoscopic vision - (स्टे'रिअस्कोपिक् व्हि'झ्यन्) **त्रिमिती संवेदन/अंतराचे/ खोलीचे दृष्टिसंवेदन** : the perception of depth or distance due to merging of two slightly different images formed on the retina of each eye.

stereotactic neurosurgesy - (स्टे'रिअटॅं'क्टिक् न्युरॉ'स'ऽजरि) **मेंदूक्षेत्रवेधी मानसशल्यक्रिया** : a refined method of psychosurgery that requires only a small opening to be made in patient's skull.

stereotype - (स्टे'रिअटाइप्) **साचेबंद पूर्वग्रह** : social perception's of an individual in terms of some readily available features like skin colour or gender, instead of personal attributes.

stimulants - (स्टि'म्युलन्ट्स्) **उत्तेजके** : psychoactive drugs that increase arousal.

stimulus - (स्टि'म्युलस्) **उद्दिपक** : an internal or external event which generates nervous system activity or response.

stranger anxiety - (स्टे'न्जऽ ऑन्झा'इअटि) **परक्या व्यक्तीमुळे वाटणारी चिंता** : the distress exprienced by a child when approached by a stranger.

stream of consciousness - (स्ट्रीम् अव्ह् कॉं'न्शस्निस्) **जाणिवेचा प्रवाह :** the continuous nature of one's conscious experience.

stress - (स्ट्रेस) **ताण :** a state of physiological or psychological tension produced due to mismatch between demands of situation and coping ability.

stress interview - (स्ट्रेस इं'न्ट'व्ह्यू) **तणाव मुलाखत :** the form of interview in which the interviewee has to fire the questions that create stress.

stress management - (स्ट्रेस में'निज्मन्ट्) **ताणाचे व्यवस्थापन :** the attempt to cope with stress through reduction of stress response.

stressor - (स्ट्रेसुऽ) **तणावजनक प्रसंग :** an event which triggers the stress response because it throws the body out of balance and compels it to respond.

stroboscopic effect - (स्ट्रोबोस्कोपीक इफे'क्ट) **सातत्याभास परिणाम :** a visual illusion of movement produced by a rapid succession of stationary images, as in films.

stroking - (स्ट्रोऽकिन्) **काळजी वाहणे/गोंजारणे :** caring recognition of and attention ·paid to another person.

Strong vocational interest blank - (स्ट्रॉन् व्होऽके'शनल् इं'न्ट्रस्ट् ब्लॉं'क्) **स्ट्रॉंग व्यावसायिक अभिरुची कसोटी :** the questionnaire about a person's interest in different vocations, designed by Strong.

structuralism - (स्ट्रि'क्चऽरॅलिझ्म्) **रचनावाद :** the school of psychology associated with wundt, which emphasises the contents of mind appearing in introspection and mental structure that contains the contents.

structured interview - (स्ट्रि'क्चऽ इं'न्ट'व्ह्यू) **संरचित मुलाखत :** an interview where the questions are arranged and planned systematically to bring out information from the interviewee.

subconscious - (सं'ब्कॉं'न्शस्) **पूर्वबोध :** something that is not quite conscious but can readily be made so.

subjective - (सब्जे'क्टिव्ह) **व्यक्तिनिष्ठ :** something existing inside oneself and not capable of being experienced by others.

sublimation - (सं'ब्लिमेऽशन्) **उदात्तीकरण :** a defence mechanism in which an acceptable unconscious impulses are channelled into consciously acceptable forms.

subliminal - (सब्लि'मिन्ल्) **अवसिमीय संवेदन :** stimuli below limen or below threshold of conscious perception.

suggestive - dream - (सजे'स्टिव्ह् ड्रीम्) **सूचक स्वप्न** : the dream which is supposed to hint at some future event.

super ego - (स्यू'पऽ/सू'-ई'गोऽ) **परमाहम्** : part if the mind, concerned with moral issues.

superior intelligence - (स्यूपि'अरिअ इन्टे'लिजन्स्) **कुशाग्र बुद्धिमत्ता** : general mental ability equivalent to or exceeding 120 IQ.

superstitions - (स्यू'पऽस्टि'शन्स) **लोकभ्रम** : false beliefs created in people due to blind faith.

surface trait - (स'ऽफिस् ट्रेऽ) **दर्शनी गुणघटक** : frequently appearing trait in person's behaviour which has emerged out of some source trait.

surrogate person - (सं'रगिट् प'ऽसन्) **पर्यायी/बदली व्यक्ती/जागा घेणारी व्यक्ती** : a person taking place of another person, psychologically.

survey research - (स'ऽव्हे रिस'ऽच्) **सर्वेक्षण संशोधन** : a technique of gathering data from large number of people by the use of questionnaires and taking samples.

sweet lemon reaction - (स्वीट्-ले'मन् रिअँ'क्शन्) **मधुर-लिंबू प्रतिक्रिया** : a form of defence mechanism by which one expresses satisfaction over whatever small thing achieved as against big expectation.

symbolic leader - (सिम्बॉ'लिक् लिडर) **प्रतिकात्मक नेता** : the leader with no power in his hand but honoured as a matter of tradition.

sympathetic branch - (सि'म्पथे'टिक् ब्राऽन्च्) **सहानुकंपी शाखा** : the part of autonomic nervous system which activates internal organs relating to emotional experience.

sympathy - सि'म्पथि) **सहानुभूती** : the ability to feel with someone.

symptom - (सि'म्टम्) **लक्षण** : an indicator of an underlying pathological condition.

synapse - (सिनॅप्स) **नसबंध** : the extremely small gaps between adjacent neurons.

syndrome - (सि'न्ड्रोम्) **संलक्षण** : a set of symptoms that are generally found together.

synoptic knob - (सिनॉ'प्टिक नॉब्) **चेतासंधी बोंड** : small swelling at the end of axon branches that enclose synoptic vescicles containing neurotransmitters.

synoptic vescicle - (सिनॉ'प्टिक व्हे'सिक्ल्) **चेतासंधी पुटिका :** small spherical or irregularly shaped structures within a synoptic terminal that contain nenrotransmitters.

systematic desensitisation therapy - (सिस्टमॅ'टिक डिसेंसिटायझेशन थे'रपि) **पद्धतशीर अवेदनशीलन पद्धती :** a form of treatment for phobia, in which the fear response to threating stimuli is replaced by different response such as muscle relaxation.

Systematic observation - (सिस्टमॅ'टिक ऑ'ब्झव्हे'ऽशन्) **पद्धतशीर निरीक्षण:** planned observation for obtaining detailed information about animal or human behaviour.

■

Taboo - (टबू') **निषेध/प्रतिबंधक** : behaviour that is forbidden by a culture.

tachistoscope - (टॅचिस्टॉस्कोप) **अल्पकालदर्शी** : an instrument for the brief exposure of words, symbols, pictures etc., visually presented material.

task-leader - (टा'ऽस्क ली'ऽडऽ) **क्रियाकेंद्री नेता/प्रशासकीय नेता** : the leader who tries to keep the attention of the group on its task and sees that the job gets done.

taste buds - (टेऽस्ट् बंडस्) **रुचिकलिका** : receptors for taste located in clusters on the tongue and around the mouth.

teaching machine (टी'चिन्ग् मशी'न्) **अध्यापन यंत्र** : an instrument for aiding programmed learning.

technophobia - (टेक्नॉफो'बिअ) **तंत्रज्ञानाचे भय** : phobia about technology.

telegraphic period - (टेलिग्रॉ'फिक् पि'अरिअड्) **तारायंत्र अवस्था** : stage of language development where children drop other parts of speech except nouns & verbs.

telekinesis - (टेलिकायनेसिस) **मन:प्रभाव गती** : moving the objects by power of mind, a parapsychological ability.

telepathy- (टेलिपथी) **दूरमनोसंप्रेषण** : communication between two minds without the aid of known senses.

temperament - (टे'म्परॅमन्ट) **स्वभावधर्म** : an individual's characteristic mood, sensitivity to stimulation and energy level.

temporal lobes - (टे'म्परल् लोऽब्ज्) **कुंभखंड** : part of brain located at the level of ears and concerned mainly with auditory functions.

tender minded - (टे'न्डड मा'इन्डिड्) **हळव्या/मृदु मनाचा/आदर्शवादी :** a personality dimension implying idealistic optimistic and spiritual outlook.

territoriality - (टे'रिटॉ'ऊरिअलिटी) **प्रादेशिकता :** the innate tendency in animals, by which they stake out territory defend it for their own use or of their group.

test battery - (टेस्ट् बॉ'टरि) **कसोटी मालिका :** a collection of tests whose composite scores are used to appraise individual differences.

testes - (टे'स्टिस्) **वृषणग्रंथी :** the male sex-glands.

testosterone - (टेस्टोस्टेरॉन) a male hormone.

test-retest reliability - (टेस्ट् रि'टेस्ट् रि'लाइअबि'लिटि) **कसोटी-पूनर्कसोटी विश्वसनीयता :** the consistency of a test when given over successive occasions to the same person.

texture gradient - (टे'क्स्चड ग्रे'ऽडिअन्ट्) **तपशीलाच्या स्पष्टतेमधील/पोतामधील सातत्यपूर्ण परिवर्तन :** continual change in fineness of details or texture.

thalamus - (थॅलॅमस्) **चेताक्षेपक :** part of brain structure located above brain - stem and working as sensory relay station and part of limbic system.

thanatology - (थनॅटोलॉजी) **मृत्यूविज्ञान :** the study of the way people deal with death & dying.

Thanatos - (थनॅटस्) **मरण-प्रवृत्ती :** Freudian concept of death force or tendency towards self-destruction.

the door in the face technique - **महत्तम लघुतम तंत्र:** the two step compliance technique in which after having a large request refused, the influencer counteroffers a much smaller request.

thematic apperception test - (थि'मॅटिक् अपरसेप्शन् टेस्ट्) **कथावस्तू अंतर्बोध कसोटी :** a projective technique developed by Murray to diagnose areas of emotional conflict of the subject with the help of the story emerged from subject's response to ambiguous & vague drawings.

theory - (थि'अरि) **मानसशास्त्रीय उपपत्ती :** (psychological) statement made for the explanation of an event or behaviour.

therapeutics - (थेराप्युटिक्स) **मनोरुग्णोपचारशास्त्र :** branch of medicine concerned with treatment and cure of disease or abnormal conditions

therapy - (थे'रपि) **मानस-उपचार पद्धती** : the use of psychological techniques to treat psychological disturbances.

thinking - (थिंकिंग्) **विचारप्रक्रिया** : the ability to imagine and represent objects or events in memory and to operate on these representations.

third force - (थऽड् फॉऽस) **तिसरी मानव्यवादी शक्ती** : psychologists who subscribe to a broadly humanistic view.

threshold - (थ्रे'शहोऽल्ड्) **सीमामूल्य** : the point on which a stimulus can be picked up by the sense-organs.

thyroid gland - (था'इअरॉइड् ग्लँड) **कंठस्थ ग्रंथी** : endocrine gland located at the neck, whose hormone determines metatolic rate.

timbre - (टि'म्बऽ) **स्वरविशेष नाद** : the quality distinguishing a tone of a given pitch sounded by one instrument form that sounded by the other.

time error : (टाईम ए'रऽ) **कालप्रमाद** : error which arises from and affects the reactions due to the order of presenting the stimuli.

time-management - (टा'इम्-मँ'निज्मन्ट्) **वेळेचे व्यवस्थापन** : planning time table for better and effective performance.

tip of the tongue phenomenon - (टिप् अव्ह् दि टंग् फिनॉ'मिनन्) **ओठावरची गोष्ट** : the failure to recall something we know well which is on the 'tip of tongue'.

tissue - (टि'श्यू) **पेशीजाल / चेताउती** : groups of neurons specialised for definite functions.

toddler - (टॉ'ड्ल्ऽ) **द्वितीय वर्षाचे बालक** : second year life span of a child.

tolerance - (टॉ'लरन्स्) **सहिष्णुता** : the need to take more and more of drug to achieve the same effect.

top down processing - (टॉप् डाउन् प्रसे'सिन्ग्) **उर्ध्वतल संस्करण** : processing that is affected by expectations and prior knowledge.

topographic model - (टपॉ'ग्रफिक मॉ'डल) **जीवनावकाशातील स्थानदर्शक प्रारूप** : Freud's model of human mind containing the conscious, preconscious and unconscious.

tough minded - (टफ् मा'इन्डिड्) **कणखर मनाची/जडवादी** : a personality dimension which implies a materialistic, pessimistic and un-spiritual outlook.

trace- decay - (ट्रेऽस् डिकेऽ) **स्मृतीचिन्हाचा ऱ्हास** : the physical disappearance of a memory trace.

trait - (ट्रेऽ) **गुणघटक** : an enduring characteristic of a person.

tranquilliser - (ट्रॅं'न्क्विं'लाइझऽ) **शांतक औषध** : a drug that reduces anxiety and agitation.

transactive analysis - (ट्रॅन्झॅं'क्टिव्ह् अनॅं'लिसिस्) **आंतरक्रियाकारी विश्लेषण:** a group therapy which examines interrelationships of group members in terms of their transactions as 'parent' 'child' or 'adult'.

transcendental meditation - (ट्रॅं'न्सन्डे'न्टल् मे'डिटे'ऽशन्) **अतितवादी चिंतन/ भावातीत ध्यान** : a technique to reach an altered state of consciousness by relaxation and meditation on a 'mantra'.

transfer of training - (ट्रॅन्स्फऽ अव्ह् ट्रेऽनिंग) **अध्ययन-संक्रमण** : learning achieved in one situation is transferred to another situation, either positively or negatively.

transference - (ट्रॅं'न्फरन्स) **भावसंक्रमण** : the transfer of patient's strong feelings for one or both parents on to the therapist during psychoanalysis.

transformational leader - (ट्रॅं'न्सफमे'ऽशनल ली'डऽ) **परिवर्तनवादी नेता** : a leader who changes the outlook and behaviour of followers.

translative memory - (ट्रॅन्स्ले'ऽटिव्ह मे'मरि) **सामुदायिक स्मृती** : a collectively shared memory system.

transsexuality - (ट्रॅं'न्ससे'क्शुऑ'लिटि) **लिंगांतरभाव** : somebody's feelings that he or she is really a member of opposite sex in the wrong body.

trauma - (ट्रॉ'ऽमऽ) **धक्का/आघात** : a physical or psychological shock resulting from injury or violence.

trial and error learning - (ट्राऽइअल् अन्ड् ए'रऽ थि'अरि) **प्रयत्न-प्रमाद अध्ययन** : a step-by-step learning over many-trails in which errors are reduced and skill is achieved.

trichromatic theory - (ट्राइक्रॉं'मॅटिक थि'अरी) **त्रिवर्ण सिद्धान्त** : theory of colour perception that postulates three basic colour receptors: red, green & blue.

trichromatism - (ट्राइक्रॉं'मॅटिझम्) **सर्वसामान्य रंगदृष्टी** : normal colour vision based on three colour systems black white, blue yellow and red-green explaining satisfactorily colour-blindness phenomenon.

truth drug - (ट्रुथ् ड्रग्) **सत्यशोधक औषधी** : a narcotic that has the effect of causing drowsiness and reducing inhibition so that the subject may reveal information that he or she would not do if fully conscious.

T-test - (टी-टेस्ट) **टी - कसोटी** : in statistics, a test for deciding whether the means of two groups of scores are significantly different.

tutorial training - (ट्यूटॉ'अरिअल् ट्रेऽनिंग्) **पंतोजीची शिकवणी/पारंपरिक अध्ययनपद्धती** : a traditional approach in which the teacher imparts knowledge to fairly passive students.

two factor theory of emotions - (टू फॅ'क्टऽ थि'अरि अव् इमो'ऽशन्) **भावनेची द्विघटक उपपत्ती** : theory which mentions physiological arousal and cognitive labelling of the cause of arousal as two factors of emotional experience.

two step flow of communication - (टू स्टेप् फ्लॉ अव् कम्यू'निके'ऽशन) **संप्रेषण वहनाचे दोन टप्पे** : mass media of communication first influence the opinion leader who in turn influence the opinions and attitudes of others.

type A personality - (टाईप ए प'ऽसनॅ'लिटि) **तणावग्रस्त (अधीरे) व्यक्तिमत्त्व प्रकार** : a personality type where type A's are typically impatient, time pressured, hostile and particularly subject to stress.

type B-personality - (टाईप बी-प'ऽसनॅ'लिटि) **संथ(धीमे) व्यक्तिमत्त्व प्रकार** : a personality type where type Bs are more relaxed and feel less pressure.

∎

unconditional positive regard - (ॲन्कन्डि'शन्ल् पॉ'झिटिव्ह रिगा'ऽड्) **बिनशर्त सकारात्मक स्वीकार** : the attitude to acceptance which the therapists has to show towards the client for successful treatment.

unconditional positive self-concept - (ॲन्कन्डि'शनल् पॉ'झिटिव्ह सेल्फ्-कॉ'न्सेप्ट) **बिनशर्त धनात्मक स्व-संकल्पना** : individual's favourable image about oneself in spite of one's short-comings.

unconditioned reflex - (ॲन्कन्डि'शन्ड् री'फ्लेक्स्) **अनभिसंधित प्रतिक्षेप** : the reflex that has not been learned previously in conditioning process.

unconditioned response - (ॲन्कन्डि'शन्ड् रिस्पॉ'न्स) **अनभिसंधित प्रतिक्रिया:** the response produced by a given stimulus at the beginning of the conditioning procedure.

unconditioned stimulus - (ॲन्कन्डि'श्नड् स्टि'म्युलस्) **अनभिसंधित उद्दिपक:** a stimulus which produces unconditioned response at the beginning of conditioning procedure.

unconscious - (ॲन्कॉ'न्शस्) **अबोधमन / नेणीव** : the region of psyche according to Freud which contains impulses and desires inhibited from entering the consciousness.

unconscious memory - (ॲन्कॉ'न्शस् मे'मरी) **अबोध स्मृती** : memories that have been forced out of the conscious level of mind into the unconscious.

unconscious motivation - (ॲन्कॉ'न्शस् मो'ऽटिव्हेऽशन्) **सुप्त/अबोध प्रेरणा:** any motivation whose origin or experience a person is unaware.

under-achiever - (ॲ'न्डऽ-अची'व्हऽ) **अव-संपादनशील** : one who fails to meet the level of achievement expected of him or her.

undoing - (अन्डू'इन्ग्) **(अवांच्छित स्मृती आणि विचार) नेस्तनाबूत करणे :** the process whereby the unconscious mind seeks to wipe out painful thoughts and memories.

unhealthy communication - (अ'न्हे'ल्थि कम्यू'निके'ऽशन) **अहितकारक अप्रभावी/मारक संप्रेषण :** the type of communication which is not congenial to better social relationship.

unilateral - (यू'निलॅ'टरल्) **एकांगी/एका बाजूचे :** affecting or pertaining to one side.

unlearned behaviour - (अन्ल'ऽन्ड् बिहे'ऽव्हऽ) **अनधित वर्तन :** the behaviour that does not depend on practice or experience for its appearance.

unobstrusive procedure - (अनआब्स्ट्रुसिव्ह प्रसी'जऽ) **नकळत तथ्य-संकलन:** a research technique for gathering data without the individual or individuals becoming aware of the procedure.

unstructured interview - (अ'न्स्ट्र'क्चऽ इ'न्ट'व्ह्यू) **अरचित मुलाखत :** the interview in which topics to be covered are unspecified and depend on unfolding reactions therein.

upper threshold - (अ'पऽ थे'श्होऽल्ड्) **उच्चतर सीमामूल्य :** upper bound of sensitivity for a particular stimulus dimension.

■

valence - (व्हॅ'लन्स्) **आकर्षकता :** psychological attractiveness of objects.

validity - (व्हॅलि'डिटी) **वैधता :** the extent to which something is true and relevant to other situations apart from study situation.

value - (व्हॅ'ल्यू) **मूल्य :** enduring belief about important life goals.

value education - (व्हॅ'ल्यू ए'ड्युकेऽशन्) **मूल्यशिक्षण :** an aspect of education focusing on specific instruction about moral values in society.

variable - (व्हे'अरिअब्ल्) **परिवर्त्य :** a condition or factor which undergoes change or changes other factors.

variable error - (व्हे'अरिअब्ल् ए'रऽ) **परिवर्तनीय प्रमाद :** error which occurs due to change in decision when a number of reactions are under study.

varience - (व्हे'अरिअन्स्) **प्रचरण :** the square of a standard deviation.

vocabulary test - (व्हऽकॅ'ब्युलरि टेस्ट) **शब्दसंग्रह कसोटी :** a test designed to assess the number of words that a person can use or understand.

verbal apraxia - (व्ह'ऽब्ल् ॲप्रेक्सिया) **वाचाजडत्व :** impaired control of proper sequencing of muscles used in speech causing laboured speech

verbal deprivation theory - (व्ह'ऽब्ल् डे'प्रिव्हेऽशन् थे'अरी) **भाषिक-वंचितता उपपत्ती :** the theory that language development is determined by social environment and deprivation of verbal social stimuli affects cognitive development.

verbal intelligence - (व्ह'ऽब्ल् इन्टे'लिजन्स्) **शाब्दिक बुद्धिमत्ता :** the ability to deal effectively with words and symbols.

verbal learning - (व्हॅ'ऽबल् ल'ऽनिंग्) **शाब्दिक अध्ययन** : learning the uses of words.

verbosity - (व्हऽबॉ'ऽसिटि) **वाचाळता** : the tendency to be excessively wordy in conversation.

vertical mobility - (व्ह'ऽटिक्ल् मो'ऽबिलिटि) **उर्ध्वचलन** : the movement of an individual towards upper socio-economic class.

vicarious learning - (व्हिके'ऽअरिअस् ल'ऽनिंग्) **प्रतिस्थापित अध्ययन** : learning by observing the behaviour of others and noting its consequences.

vipashyana - (विपश्यना) **विपश्यना** : a zen Buddhistic technique for meditation in which the meditator attempts to control the senses and mind with open eyes.

visual spatial sketch pad - (व्हि'इ्युअल स्पे'ऽशल स्केच् पॅड्) **दृश्य अवकाशात्मक रेखाटन स्थान** : a system within working memory designed for spatial and visual coding .

visual acuity - (व्हि'इ्युअल् ॲक्युटी) **दृष्टितीक्ष्णता** : the ability to detect visual details.

visual agnosia - (व्हि'इ्युअल् अग्नोशिया) **प्रत्यभिज्ञाभाव** : a disorder where individual sees but fails to recognize objects.

visual buffer - (व्हि'इ्युअल् बॅफऽ) **दृष्टिवेदनात्मक स्मृतीसंस्करणअवस्था** : visual representation of verbal and non-verbal items in encoding process of short term memory.

visual cliff - (व्हि'इ्युअल् क्लिफ्) **दर्शनीखाई** : an apparatus used to study the existence of depth perception in humans and animals.

visual constancies - (व्हि'इ्युअल् कॉ'न्स्टन्सिज्) **दृष्टिसांवेदनिक सातत्य** : that object's size, shape, colour etc. are perceived as remaining constant regardless of variation in retinal image.

visual cortex - (व्हि'इ्युअल् कॉऽटेक्स्) **मेंदूपृष्ठातील दृष्टिक्षेत्र** : part of cerebral cortex dedicated to vision, located in the occipital lobe.

visual dominance - (व्हि'इ्युअल् डॉ'मिनन्स्) **दृष्टिवेदनवर्चस्व** : that vision is usually dominant amongst conflicting stimuli from different sensory modalities.

visual field - (व्हि'इ्युअल् फील्ड्) **दृष्टिक्षेत्र** : the total visual array acting on eye when it is directed towards a fixation point.

visual search - (व्हि'झ्युअल् स॒ऽच्) **दृक शोधन** : a task in which visual target must be located quickly from among distractors.

visual spatial coding - (व्हि'झ्युअल् स्पे'ऽशल को'ऽडिन्ग्) **दृश्य अवकाशात्मक संकेतन** : the memory's way of automatically encoding information by its appearance.

vocational counseling - (व्होऽके'शनल् का'उन्सलिंग्) **व्यावसायिक सहयंत्रणा** : couseling as applied to the problems of vocational adjustment.

vocational education - (व्हो'के'शनल् ए'ज्युके'ऽशन्) **व्यावसायिक प्रशिक्षण** : training designed to fit a person for a particular job or profession.

volition - (व्हलि'शन्) **संकल्प** : Conscious, voluntary selection of particular action.

voluntary attention - (व्हॉ'लन्टरि अटे'न्शन्) **ऐच्छिक अवधान** : the type of attention given to an object or event willingly and out of internal urge.

volunteer bias - (व्हॉ'लन्टि'अ बा'इअस्) **स्वयंसेवी-प्रयुक्ताविषयीचा पूर्वग्रह** : the self - selected participants are highly motivated to perform better than people selected at random, in the research.

Vygotasky test - (व्हिगोटस्की टेस्ट्) **व्हिगोटस्की कसोटी** : a test of ability to form concepts.

W

warming up period - (वॉ'ऽमिन् अॅप् पि'अरिअड्) **कार्यप्रवणतेचा काळ :** Initial stage in learning in which movements & responses are inexact and tentative in spite of familiarity with the task.

we - group - (वी ग्रूप्) **समूह** the group for the individual whose members express ideas, goals and feelings similar to his own.

weapons effect - (वे'पन्स् इफे'क्ट्) **शस्त्रदर्शनाचा उत्तेजन परिणाम :** increase in aggressive behaviour caused by mere sight of weapon.

Weber's law - (वेबर्स लॉ) **वेबरचा नियम :** a law about relativity of one's judgement of stimulus sensation stating that the just noticeable difference between two stimuli is a constant proportion of original stimulus.

Wechsler adult intelligence Scale (WAIS) - (वेश्लर अडं'ल्ट् इन्टे'लिजन्स् स्केऽल्) **वेश्लर प्रौढ बुद्धिमत्ता कसोटी :** the intelligence tests for adults combining performance and verbal ability testing.

Wechster intelligence scale for children (WISC) - (वेश्लर इन्टे'लिजन्स् स्केऽल् फॉऽ चि'ल्ड्रन्) **बालकांसाठी वेश्लर बुद्धिमत्ता कसोटी :** a modification of wechsler adult intelligence scale, used for adolescent and older children.

weight set point - (वेऽट् सेट् पॉइन्ट) **वजनाचा स्थितबिंदू :** particular level of weight maintained by the body.

Wernic's aphasia - (वेर्निक्स अॅफेशिया) **वेर्निकची भाषा अक्षमता :** speech disorder involving wrong choice of words.

Wernicke's area - (वेर्निक्स् ए'अरिअ) **वेर्निक वाचा क्षेत्र :** the area of cerebral cortex which is concerned with the processing of speech sounds into recognisable language.

whole method - (होऽल् मे'थड्) **अखंड/समग्र पद्धती** : a technique for learning in which the material is learned as a whole on each practice or repetition.

wish fulfilment - (विश् फुल्फि'ल्मन्ट्) **स्वप्नाधारित इच्छापूर्ती** : in psychoanalysis, an attempt to fulfil an impulse or desire usually by fantasy or in dreams.

wishful thinking - (वि'शफुल् थिंकिंग्) **इच्छानुगामी विचार** : thinking according to one's wishes and desires rather than directed by objective constrains or reality.

withdrawal symptoms - (विद्ड्राॅ'ऽअल् सि'म्टम्) **माघार लक्षणे** : the physical or psychological effects of no longer taking a substance to which one has become addicted

withdrawal - (विद्ड्राॅ'ऽअल्) **माघार प्रवृत्ती** : removing oneself from conflicting situation and resorting to alcohol, drugs, sex or even work.

withdrawal delirium - (विद्ड्राॅ'ऽअल् डिलि'रिअम्) **माघारजन्य विभ्रम** : delirium which is caused by the withdrawal of a drug upon which one had built up severe dependence.

word association test - (वऽड् असो'ऽशिएऽशन् टेस्ट्) **शब्द-साहचर्य कसोटी** : a test where the subject is asked to give immediate response to a list of pre-selected words, for probing person's repressed impulses.

work places stressor - (व'ऽक् प्लेससेस् स्ट्रेसर) **कार्यस्थळ तणावजन्य घटक** : factors in the work environment or aspects of job that cause stress.

work psychology - (व'ऽक् साइकाॅ'लजि) **कार्मिक मानसशास्त्र** : the branch of psychology dealing with job related factors such as selection, training, job satisfaction and human relationships in the job and to the machines.

working memory - (व'ऽकिन्ग् मे'मरि) **प्रवर्तक स्मृती/कार्यरत स्मृती** : it is that memory which emphasises the active, task-based nature of the store.

working through - (व'ऽकिन्ग् थ्रू) **समस्याभेदन-क्षमता-संपादन** : a process of psychotherapy in which patient, incourse of treatment gains same insight into his problems and achieves ability to cope with similar situations independently.

■

X

x -chromosome - (एक्स क्रॉमसॉम) **क्ष-रंगसूत्र :** a chromosome which determines maleness if paired with Y and femaleness if paried with X.

X -X - (एक्स् एक्स्) **स्त्रीलिंग-निर्धारक रंगसूत्र :** normal genotype pattern for a human female in which two sex chromosomes have been present.

Xenophobia - (झे'नफोऽबिअ) **अपरिचित व्यक्तीचे भय :** a phobia about strangers.

XXX - syndrome - (एक्स् एक्स् एक्स् सि'न्ड्रोम) **स्त्रीवाचक संलक्षण :** phenotypically female with three X-chromosomes, with menstrual problems.

XXXY - syndrome - (एक्स् एक्स् एक्स् वाइ सि'न्ड्रोम) **क्लाइनफेल्टर संलक्षणाचा भिन्न प्रकार :** a variant of Klinefelter's syndrome.

XXY - syndrome - (एक्स् एक्स् वाइ सि'न्ड्रोम) **क्लाइनफेल्टर संलक्षण :** genetic abnormality characterized by mental retardation and tendency towards femininity, (known as Klinefeltor's syndrome)

XY - (एक्स् वाइ) **पुरुष-लिंग निर्धारक रंगसूत्र :** normal genotype pattern for human male having two sex-chromosomes.

XYY- syndrome - (एक्स् वाइ वाइ सि'न्ड्रोम) **पुरुषवाचक संलक्षण :** an anomaly in which persons having three chromosomes are phenotypically male with very low fertility.

XYZ pattern - (एक्स् वाइ झेड् पॅ'टर्न्) **गुन्हेगारी/आक्रमकता प्रवृत्तीवाचक :** a genetic abnormality which is believed to be related to criminal or aggressive behaviour.

■

Y

Y - chromosome - (वाइ-क्रॉमसॉम) **य-रंगसूत्र** : the chromosome which combined with X chromosome determines maleness of the individual.

y - maze - (वाइ मेऽझ्) **वाय-व्यूह** : a maze shaped like the letter Y, having a single approach alley and two arms one of which the subject must choose.

yellow spot - (ये'लोऽ स्पॉट्) **पीत-बिंदू** : a small area which lies in central posterior section of the retina.

Yerks Dodson law - (यर्कस् डॉडसन लॉ) **यर्कस् डॉडसन नियम** : the law which states that the performance is highest at a medium level of arousal, and is very poor when the arousal level is very low or very high.

yes - no question - (येस्-नो-क्वे'स्चन्) **होय-नाही प्रश्न** : the term used for any interrogative that takes either 'yes' or 'no' as the prescribed answer.

yoga - (योगा) **अमूर्त तत्त्वचिंतनाचे तंत्र/योग** : formalised techniques of abstract contemplation developed by Indian philosophers.

Young Helm Holts theory - (यंग हेल्महोल्ट्झ थिअरी) **यंत्र-हेल्महोल्ट्झ (रंगविषयक) उपपत्ती** : theory of colour vision which suggests three colour receptors - red, green & blue and that all other colours are reducible to some combination of these three.

youth - (यूथ) **युवावस्था/किशोरावस्था** : defined as the period between childhood and maturity.

■

zeigarnic effect - (झायगर्निक इफेक्ट) **झायगर्निक परिणाम :** the finding by Zeigarnik that details of interrupted task are more remembered than those of completed tasks.

zeitgeist - (झीटगीस्ट) **युगधर्म/कालमहिमा :** denotes the 'spirit of times' which affects the emotional and mental life of everyone who lives through the era,

zener cards - (झिनर कार्ड्स्) **झेनर कार्ड्स् :** a deck of cards used in research on extrasensory perception.

zero sum game - (झि'अरोऽ सम् गेऽम्) **एकाची हानि, तोच दुसऱ्याचा लाभ** a situation where one person's losses are another's gains because there is finite amount to be won.

zero transfer - (झि'अरोऽ ट्रान्सफर) **शून्य संक्रमण :** no transfer of learning from one learning situation to another.

zollner illusion - (झोलनर इल्यूशन) **झोलनरचा भ्रम :** a visual illusion in which parallel lines appear to diverge.

zone of proximal development - (झो'न् अव्ह् प्रॉ'क्सिमल् डिव्हे'लप्मेन्ट्) **क्षमतांच्या पूर्णाविष्काराची निकट-पूर्व स्थिती :** the capacities which are being developed but are not yet functioning fully, according to Vygotsky's theory.

zoomorphism - (झूमॉ'ऽफिझम्) **अमानवीकरण, पाशवी गुणारोपण** the interpretation of human behaviour in terms appropriate to animal behaviour.

zoophobia - (झूफोबिया) **प्राणिभय :** the phobia about animals.

zygote - (झायगोट) **फलित पेशी :** the cell formed by the union of the sperm cell and the egg cell of parents from which new individual develops. ■

परिशिष्ट १
काही मानसिक विकृतीवाचक संज्ञा
(Terms related to mental disorders)

acrophobia (अॅक्रोफोबिया) - उंच जागेचे भय

acarophobia (अकॅरोफोबिया) - कीटकभय

adromania (अॅड्रोमॅनिया) - स्त्री-कामोन्माद

aerophobia (एरोफोबिया) - उंच जागांचे भय

agnosia (अॅग्नोशिया) - प्रत्यभिज्ञाभाव, अर्थ-आकलन अक्षमता

agorophobia (अॅगॉरोफोबिया) - खुल्या जागेचे भय

aichonophobia (ऐकोनोफोबिया) - अणकुचीदार वस्तूंचे भय

ailurophobia (एल्युरोफोबिया) - मांजराचे भय

alexia (अॅलेक्शिया) - वाचन अक्षमता

algophobia (अल्गोफोबिया) - वेदनाभय

azheimers' disease (अल्झायमर्स डिसीज्) - वार्धक्य विस्मृतीरोग

amaxophobia (अमॅक्झोफोबिया) - वाहन भय

amnesia (Infantile) (अॅम्नेशिया (इन्फन्टाइल) - शिशुकालचा स्मृतीलोप

anaclitic depression (अॅनॅक्लिटिक डिप्रेशन) - मातृविरहजन्य खिन्नताविकृती

anorexia nervosa (अॅनोरेक्शिया नर्व्होसा) - क्षुधाभाव चेतापदशा

anthrophobia (अॅन्थ्रोफोबिया) - माणूसभय, समाजभय

aphasia (अॅफेशिया) - भाषिक अक्षमता

arachnophobia (अॅरॅक्नोफोबिया) - कोळ्या कीटकांचे भय

astraphobia (अॅस्ट्राफोबिया) - वादळ-विजांचे भय

bipolar disorder (बायपोलर डिसऑर्डर) - द्विध्रुवीय भावनिक विकृती

bulimia nervosa (ब्युलिमिया नर्व्होसा) - क्षुधातिरेक चेतापदशा

bacillophobia (बॅसिलोफोबिया) - जंतुभय

bibliophobia (बिब्लिओफोबिया) - ग्रंथभय

claustrophobia (क्लॅस्ट्रोफोबिया) - बंदिस्त जागेचे भय

catalepsy (कॅटॅलेप्सी)	-	स्नायुताठरता
cataplexy (कॅटॅप्लेक्सी)	-	भयाने थिजणे
conduction aphasia (कंडक्शन अफेशिया)	-	संवहन-भाषिक अक्षमता
cyberphobia (सायबरफोबिया)	-	संगणक भय
conversion hysteria (कन्व्हर्शन हिक्टेरिया)	-	रूपांतरणात्मक उन्माद
cynophobia (सायनोफोबिया)	-	कुत्र्याचे भय
dancing mania (डान्सिंग मॅनिया)	-	नृत्योन्माद
delusion of grandeur (डिल्यूजन ऑफ ग्रॅंजर)	-	थोरत्व विभ्रम
delusion of persecution (डिल्यूजन ऑफ पर्सिक्युशन)	-	छळ-विभ्रम
dementia (डिमेन्शिया)	-	अवमनस्कता
depression (डिप्रेशन)		खिन्नताविकृती/अवसादावस्था
demophobia (डिमोफोबिया)	-	जमावभय
dissociative disorder (डिसोशिएटिव्ह डिसऑर्डर)	-	वियोजनात्मक विकृती
dissociative hysteria (डिसोशिएटिव्ह हिस्टेरिया)	-	वियोजनमूलक उन्माद
dipsomania (डिप्सॉमॅनिया)	-	मद्यपानाची सणक/अनिवार्य मद्याकर्षण
dyslexia (डिस्लेक्शिया)	-	वाचन-अक्षमता
dysphonia (डिस्फोनिया)	-	चिंतावसाद
ecolalia (इकोलॅलिया)	-	निरर्थक पुनरुच्चारण
endogenous depression (इंडोजिनस डिप्रेशन)	-	आंतरिक(कारणोभ्दव) खिन्नता
enissophobia (एनिसोफोबिया)	-	टीकाभय
enuresis (एन्यूरेसिस)	-	अनियंत्रित मूत्रविसर्जन
epilepsy (एपिलेप्सी)	-	अपस्मार
ergasiophobia (एर्गॅशिओफोबिया)	-	जबाबदारीचे भय
erotophobia (इरोटोफोबिया)	-	मैथुनभय
exhibitionism (एक्झिबिशनिझम)	-	जननेंद्रिय प्रदर्शन
experimental neurosis (एक्स्पेरिमेंटल न्यूरॉसिस)	-	प्रायोगिक नसविकृती
false memory syndrome (फॉल्स मेमरी सिंड्रम्)	-	मिथ्यास्मृती संलक्षण
fetischism (फेटिशिझम)	-	वस्तुकामिता

frigidity (फ्रिजिडिटी)	-	कामबधिरता
fugue (फ्यूग)	-	विस्मृती पलायन
functional disorder (फंक्शनल डिस्ऑर्डर)	-	कार्यिक विकृती
gamophobia (गॅमोफोबिया)	-	विवाहभय
gerontopholia (जिराँटोफोबिया)	-	जरामैथुन
glossolalia (ग्लोसोलॅलिया)	-	कृत्रिम/तुटक शब्दोच्चारण
hebephrenic, Schizophrenia (हिबिफ्रेनिक स्किझोफ्रेनिया)	-	यौवनसंलग्न, छिन्नमनस्कता
hematophobia (हेमॅटोफोबिया)	-	रक्तभय
homophobia (होमोफोबिया)	-	मानवभय
hydrophobia (हैड्रोफोबिया)	-	जलभय
hyperphagia (हायपरफॅजिया)	-	अतिक्षुधन
hyperthyroidism (हायपरथॉयरॉयडिझम्)	-	अतिक्रियाशीलता
hypochondsia (हायोकोंड्रिया)	-	रोगभ्रम
hysteria (हिस्टेरिया)	-	उन्माद-विकृती
incest (इन्सेस्ट)	-	व्यभिचारी वर्तन
infantilism (इंफटाइलिझम्)	-	बालिशवृत्ती/पोरकटपणाचे वर्तन
involutional melancholia (इन्व्होल्यूशनल मेलँकोलिया)	-	मध्यमवयीन खिन्नतावस्था
kleptomania (क्लेप्टोमॅनिया)	-	वस्तू चोरण्याची विकृती
Korsakoffs' syndrome (कोसॉकोफ्स सिंड्रम)	-	कोसॉकोफचे संलक्षण/मद्यसंलग्र स्मृतीभ्रंश
lalophobia (लॅलोफोबिया)	-	भाषणभय
lesbianism (लेस्बिऑनिझम)	-	समलिंगी कामप्रवृत्ती (स्त्रियांमधील)
mania (मॅनिया)	-	उन्मादविकृती
manic depressive (मॅनिक-डिप्रेसिव्ह)	-	उन्माद-अवसाद

masochism (मॅसोचिझम्)	- आत्मपीडनरती
masturbation (मास्टरबेशन)	- हस्तमैथुन
megalomanic (मेगॅलोमॅनिक)	- बढाईखोर वृत्तीचा
melancholia (मेलँकोलिया)	- विषण्णता
misogyny (मिसोगिनी)	- स्त्रीद्रष्टेपणा
monophobia (मोनोफोबिया)	- एकटेपणाचे भय
mysophobia (मायसोफोबिया)	- जंतूंचे भय/घाणीचे भय
narcissism (नार्सिसिझम)	- आत्मप्रीती
narcolepsy (नार्कोलेप्सी)	- अनिवार्य निद्राप्रवृत्ती
necrophilia (नेक्रोफिलिया)	- प्रेतरती
neophobia (निओफोबिया)	- नाविन्याचे भय
nectophobia (नेक्टोफोबिया)	- काळोखाचे भय
neurosis (न्यूरॉसिस)	- नसविकृती
nymphomania (निंफोमॉनिया)	- स्त्री-कामोन्माद
obsession (ऑब्सेशन)	- कल्पना अनिवार्यता
obsessive Compulsive neurosis (आब्सेसिव्ह कंपल्सीव्ह न्यूरॉसिस)	- कल्पना-कृती-अनिवार्यता नसविकृती
ocholophobia (ऑकोलोफोबिया)	- जमावभय
onomotophobia (ऑनोफोमोफोबिया)	- विशिष्ट संज्ञा भय
ophidiophobia (ऑफिडिओफोबिया)	- सर्पभय
panophobia (पॅनोफोबिया)	- सर्व-भय
pathophobia (पॅथोफोबिया)	- रोगभय
pedophilia (पिडोफिलिया)	- बालमैथुन
paranoia (पॅरॅनोइया)	- संशय-विक्षोभ-विकृती
parapraxis (पॅरॅप्रॅक्सिस)	- वर्तनप्रमाद/वाणीची गफलत
phobia (फोबिया)	- भयगंड
postpartum depression (पोस्टपार्टम् डिप्रेशन)	- प्रसूतीपश्चात खिन्नता
prosopagnosia (प्रोसोपॅग्नोशिया)	- मुद्राप्रत्याभिज्ञाभाव/चेहरा ओळखता न येणे

psychoneurosis (सायकोन्यूरॉसिस)	-	मानस नसविकृती
psychosis (सायकोसिस)	-	मनोविकृती/चेताविकृती
pyromania (पाइरोमॅनिया)	-	अग्निप्रज्वलनविकृती
pyrophobia (पाइरोफोबिया)	-	अग्निभय
sadism (सॅडिझम्)	-	परपीडनरती
sado-masochism (सॅडो-मॅसोचिझम्)	-	परपीडन-आत्मपीडनरती
satyriasis (सॅटिरिऑसिस)	-	पुरुष-कामोन्माद
schizophrenia (स्किझोफ्रेनिया)	-	छिन्नमनस्कता
scoptophilia (स्कोटोफिलिया)	-	नग्नतादर्शनरती
senile dementia (सेनाइल डिमेन्शिया)	-	वार्धक्यजन्म अवमनस्कता
somnambulism (सोम्नॅम्ब्युलिझम्)	-	निद्राभ्रमण
syphilophobia (सिफिलोफोबिया)	-	गुप्तरोगभय
taxophobia (टॅक्सोफोबिया)	-	विषबाधेचे भय
thanatophobia (थनॅटोफोबिया)	-	मृत्यूभय
thalassophobia (थलॅसोफोबिया)	-	समुद्रभय
taphophobia (टॅफोफोबिया)	-	स्मशानभय
theophobia (थिओफोबिया)	-	ईश्वरभय
technophobia (टेक्नोफोबिया)	-	तंत्रज्ञानविषयक भय
visual agnosia (व्हिजुअल ॲग्नोशिया)	-	प्रत्याभिज्ञाभाव
voyeurism (व्होयुरिझम्)	-	नग्नतादर्शनरती
xenophobia (झिनोफोबिया)	-	अपरिचित/परक्या व्यक्तीचे भय
zenoglossophobia (झिनोग्लोसोफोबया)	-	परकीय भाषाभय
zoophobia (झूफोबिया)	-	प्राणिभय

परिशिष्ट २

मानसशास्त्राच्या शाखा व इतर संबंधित शास्त्रे
(Sub-Branches of Psychology & related sciences)

abnormal psychology (ऑबनार्मल सायकॉलजि) - अपसामान्य मानसशास्त्र
aetiology (इटिओलॉजी) विकृतीमीमांसा
applied psychology (अप्लाइड सायकॉलजि) - उपयोजित मानसशास्त्र
adolescent psychology (ऑडोलेसंट सायकॉलजि)- किशोरवयीन मानसशास्त्र
anthropology (अँथ्रपोलजि) - सांस्कृतिक मानवशास्त्र

behavioral science (बिहेविअरल सायन्स) - वर्तनशास्त्र
behavioural genetics (बिहेविअरल जेनेटिक्स) - वर्तनात्मक जननशास्त्र

child psychology (चाइल्ड सायकॉलजि) - बालमानसशास्त्र
chronobiology (क्रोनोबायोलजि) - कालिक जीवशास्त्र
clinical psychology (क्लिनिकल सायकॉलजि) - चिकित्सा मानसशास्त्र
cognitive neuropsychology (कॉग्निटिव्ह
न्यूरोसॉयकॉलजि) - बोधात्मक नसमानसशास्त्र
cognitive psychology (कॉग्निटिव्ह सायकॉलजि) - बोधात्मक मानसशास्त्र
community psychology (कम्युनिटी सायकॉलजि) - जमातीचे मानसशास्त्र
comparative psychology (कम्पॅरेटिव्ह सायकॉलजि) - तुलनात्मक मानसशास्त्र
consumer psychology (कन्झ्युमर सायकॉलजि) - ग्राहक/उपभोक्ता मानसशास्त्र
cross-cultural psychology (क्रॉस कल्चरल
सायकॉलजि) - आंतर-सांस्कृतिक मानसशास्त्र
cybernetics (सायबरनेटिक्स) - मस्तिष्क संवहनशास्त्र
cognitive ergonomics (कॉग्निटिव्ह एर्गोनॉमिक्स) - मानव-संगणक तंत्रज्ञान
संबंधशास्त्र
cognitive neuroscience (कॉग्निटिव्ह न्यूरोसायन्स)- बोधात्मक नसविज्ञान
congnitive science (कॉग्निटिव्ह सायन्स) - बोधात्मक प्रक्रियांचे विज्ञान

depth psychology (डेप्थ सायकॉलॉजि) - मनोगहन मानसशास्त्र
descriptive statistics (डिस्क्रिप्टिव्ह स्टॅटिस्टिक्स) - वर्णनात्मक संख्याशास्त्र

developmental psychology (डिव्हलपमेंटल
   सायकॉलजि) - वैकासिक मानसशास्त्र
dynamic psychology (डायनॅमिक सायकॉलॉजि) - मनोगतिक मानसशास्त्र

ego psychology (इगो सायकॉलॉजि) - अहम्(विषयक) मानसशास्त्र
engineering psychology (इंजिनिअरिंग
   सायकॉलॉजी) - अभियांत्रिकी मानसशास्त्र
ergonomics (एर्गोनॉमिक्स) - मानव-यंत्र-संबंध शास्त्र
ethology (इथॉलजि) - नैसर्गिक निरीक्षणाधारित
   प्राणिवर्तनाचा अभ्यास

eugenics (युजेनिक्स) - सुप्रजाजनशास्त्र
evolutionary psychiatry (इव्होल्युशनरी
   सायकिअॅट्री) - उत्क्रांतीवादी मनोविकृती
   उपचारशास्त्र

evolutionary psychology (इव्होल्युशनरी
   सायकॉलॉजि) - उत्क्रांतीवादी मानसशास्त्र
existential psychology (एक्झिस्टेन्शियल
   सायकॉलॉजि) - अस्तित्ववादी मानसशास्त्र
experimental psychology (एक्स्पेरिमेंटल
   सायकॉलॉजि) - प्रायोगिक मानसशास्त्र

forensic psychology (फोरेन्सिक सायकॉलॉजि) - न्यायवैद्यक मानसशास्त्र

Gestalt psychology (गेस्टाल्ट सायकॉलजि) - समष्टिवादी मानसशास्त्र
graphology (ग्रॅफॉलजि) - हस्ताक्षरविद्या
group dynamics (ग्रुप डायनॅमिक्स) - समूहगतीविज्ञान

health psychology (हेल्थ सायकॉलजि) - आरोग्य मानसशास्त्र
humanistic psychology (ह्युमॅनिस्टिक सायकॉलजि) - मानव्यवादी मानसशास्त्र

industrial psychology (इन्डस्ट्रिअल सायकॉलॉजी)- औद्योगिक मानसशास्त्र
inferertial statistics (इन्फरेन्शियल स्टॅटिस्टिक्स) - निष्कर्षात्मक संख्याशास्त्र/
   अनुमानाधारित संख्याशास्त्र

Jerontology (जेरोंटॉलजि)	-	जराविज्ञान
liberal humanistic psychology (लिबरल ह्युमॅनिस्टिक सायकॉलजि	-	उदारमतवादी मानव्यवाद
naive psychology (नाइव्ह सायकॉलजि)	-	बालबोध मानसशास्त्र
neurology (न्यूरॉलजि)	-	नस (संस्था) विज्ञान
neurophysiology (न्यूरोफिजिऑलजि)	-	नस शरीर विज्ञान
neuropsychology (न्यूरोसायकॉलजि)	-	नस मानसशास्त्र
occupational psychology (ऑक्युपेशनल सायकॉलजि)	-	व्यावसायिक मानसशास्त्र
paediatrics (पीडिऑट्रिक्स)	-	बालआरोग्यविज्ञान
paleo psychology (पॅलिओ सायकॉलजि)	-	पुरातन उत्क्रांती संदर्भी मानसशास्त्र
parapsychology (पॅरासायकॉलजि)	-	परामानसशास्त्र
para lingnistics (पॅरालिंग्विस्टिक्स)	-	अभाषिक संप्रेषण घटकांचे शास्त्र
penology (पिनॉलाजि)	-	(अपराध) दंडनशास्त्र
personal psychology (पर्सनॅलिटी सायकॉलजि)	-	व्यक्तिमत्त्व मानसशास्त्र
personnel psychology (पर्सोनल सायकॉलजि)	-	कर्मचारी मानसशास्त्र
phenomenology (फिनॉमेनॉलजी)	-	घटनासंवेदनशास्त्र
phrenology (फ्रेनॉलजि)	-	मस्तिष्क विज्ञान
physiognomy (फिजिओनॉमी)	-	(मुख) मुद्रा विज्ञान
physiological psychology (फिजिओलॉजिकल सायकॉलजि)	-	शरीर मानसशास्त्र
psychobiology (सायकोबायॉलजि)	-	मानसजैवविज्ञान
psychodiagnostics (सायकोडायग्रोस्टिक्स)	-	मानसनिदानशास्त्र
psychodynamics (सायकोडायनॅमिक्स)	-	मानसगतीविज्ञानक
psychohistory (सायकोहिस्टरी)	-	इतिहास मनोविज्ञान
psycholingnistics (सायकोलिंग्विस्टिक्स)	-	मानस-भाषाविज्ञान
psychometrics (सायकोमेट्रिक्स)	-	मनोमापनशास्त्र

psycho neuro immunology (सायको न्यूरो इम्युनॉलजि)	- मानस-नस-प्रतिकारक्षमता विज्ञान
psychopathology (सायकोपॅथॉलजि)	- मनोविकृती संशोधनशास्त्र
psychopharmacology (सायको फार्मकोलजि)	- मानस औषधीशास्त्र
psychophysics (सायकोफिजिक्स)	- मानसभौतिकी
social Psychology (सोशल सायकॉलजि)	- सामाजिक मानसशास्त्र
socio biology (सोशिओबायॉलजि)	- सामाजिक जैवविज्ञान
socio-lingnistics (सोशिओ लिंग्विस्टिक्स)	- सामाजिक भाषाविज्ञान
space psychology (स्पेस सायकॉलजि)	- अंतराळ मानसशास्त्र
thanatology (थनॅटॉलजि)	- मृत्यूविज्ञान
topological psychology (टोपोलोजिकल सायकॉलजि)	- जीवनावकाशी मानसशास्त्र
work psychology (वर्क सायकॉलजि)	- कार्य मानसशास्त्र

परिशिष्ट ३

नससंस्था व संबंधित संज्ञा
(Nervous-system - related terms)

ablation (ॲब्लेशन) - मेंदूकर्तनशस्त्रक्रिया

adrenal gland (ॲड्रिनल ग्लँड) - वृक्कस्थ ग्रंथी

adrenaline (ॲड्रेनलीन) - वृक्कस्थ ग्रंथीस्राव

afferent neuron (ॲफरंट न्यूरॉन) - वेदक नसपेशी

allele (ॲलिली) - जोडीतील एक जनुक

autonomus nervous system (ऑटोनॉमस
नर्व्हस सिस्टम) - स्वायत्त नससंस्था

aphasia (अफेशिया) - भाषिक अक्षमता

associative neuron (असोशिएटिव्ह न्यूरॉन) - संयोजक नसपेशी

archnoid matter (आर्कनॉइड मॅटर) - जालमय आवरण

auditory cortex (ऑडिटरी कॉर्टेक्स) - मेंदूपृष्ठावरील श्रवणकेंद्र

axon (ॲक्झॉन) - अक्षतंतू

blind-spot (ब्लाईंड स्पॉट) - अंधबिंदू

brain dmage (ब्रेन डॅमेज) - मेंदू-क्षती

brain localisation (ब्रेन लोकलायझेशन) - मेंदूतील स्थानिकीकरण

brain potential (ब्रेन पोटेन्शियल) - मेंदूतील विद्युतक्रियापातळी

brain stimulation (ब्रेन स्टिम्युलेशन) - मेंदू-उद्दिपन

brain waves (ब्रेन वेव्हज) - मेंदू लहरी

Broca's area (ब्रोकाज एरिया) - ब्रोकाचे वाचाक्षेत्र

cat scan (कॅट स्कॅन) - संगणकीकृत अक्षीय टोमोग्राफी
निरीक्षण

central nervous system (सेंट्रल नर्व्हस सिस्टम) - केंद्रीय नससंस्था

cerebellum (सेरेबेलम) - लहान मेंदू

cerebral cortex (सेब्रिल कॉर्टेक्स) - मेंदू पृष्ठ

cerebral dominance (सेब्रिल डॉमिनन्स) - मेंदूगोलार्धाचे प्राबल्य

cerebral hemispheres (सेब्रिल हेमिस्फिअर्स) - मेंदूगोलार्ध

cerebrum (सेरेब्रम)	- मोठा मेंदू
corpus collosum (कॉर्पस् कोलोसम)	- मेंदू गोलार्धबंध/महासंयोजी पिंड
chromosome (क्रोमोझोम)	- रंगसूत्र
cybernetics (सायबरनेटिक्स)	- मस्तिष्कसंवहनशास्त्र
decortication (डिकॉर्टिकेशन)	- मेंदूपृष्ठविभक्तीकरण शस्त्रक्रिया
dendrites (डेंड्राइट्स)	- वृक्षिका
dura matter (ड्युरा मॅटर)	- ड्युरा आवरण
efferent neuron (एफरंट न्यूरॉन)	- कारक नसपेशी
electroenchophologram (इलेक्ट्रोएन्सिफोलोग्रॅम)	- विद्युतमस्तिष्कालेख
encephalitis (एन्सेफेलायटिस)	- मेंदूज्वर
epilepsy (एपिलेप्सी)	- अपस्मार
fissure of Rolando (फिशर ऑफ रोलँडो)	- रोलँडोची खाच
fissure of Sylvius (फिशर ऑफ सिल्व्हियस)	- सिल्व्हियसची खाच
functional MIR (फंक्शनल एम्आयआर)	- कार्यिक चुंबकीय अनुनाद प्रतिमादर्शन
frontal lobe (फ्रंटल लोब)	- अग्रखंड
genes (जीन्स)	- वंशाणू, जनुके
glucosates (ग्लुकोस्टॅट्स)	- रक्तशर्करामापक पेशी
hemispheric asymmetry (हेमिस्फेरिक असिमेट्री)	- मेंदूगोलार्धांची असमानता
hippocampus (हिप्पोकँप्स)	- अश्वमीन
hydrocephalus (हैड्रोसिफॅलस)	- जलशीर्षता
hypothalamus (हायपोथलॅमस)	- अधःश्चेताक्षेपक
lateralisation (लॅटरलायझेशन)	- पार्श्वीकरण
lesian (लिझन)	- (मेंदू) क्षत
limbic system (लिंबिक सिस्टम)	- किनारी संस्था
lobotomy (लोबोटॉमी)	- मेंदूखंडकर्तन शस्त्रक्रिया
medulla oblongata (मेड्युला ऑबलाँगाटा)	- लंबमज्जा

MIR scan (एमआयआर स्कॅन)	– चुंबकीय अनुनाद प्रतिमादर्शन
motor neuron (मोटर न्यूरॉन)	– कारक नसपेशी
neuroliptic drug (न्युरोलिप्टिक ड्रग)	– नसविकृतीजनक औषध
neurology (न्यूरॉलजि)	– नसविज्ञान
neuron (न्यूरॉन)	– नसपेशी
neurophysiology (न्यूरोफिजिऑलजि)	– नसशरीरशास्त्र
neurotransmitter (न्यूरोट्रान्समीटर)	– नससंवाहक
neurosis (न्युरॉसिस)	– नसविकृती
noradrenaline (नॉरअॅड्रेनलीन)	– नॉरअॅड्रेनलीन स्राव
occipital lobe (ऑक्सिपिटल लोब)	– पार्श्वखंड
old brain (ओल्ड ब्रेन)	– जुना मेंदू
olfaction (ऑल फॅक्शन)	– गंधवेदन
optic chiasma (ऑप्टिक चायझमा)	– दृष्टिनसांचा छेदनबिंदू
optic nerve (ऑप्टिक नर्व्ह)	– दृष्टिनस
parasympathetic branch (पॅरॅसिंपथेटिक ब्रँच)	– परानुकंपी शाखा
parietal lobe (पेरिएटल लोब)	– मध्यखंड
pet scan (पेट स्कॅन)	– पेट स्कॅन
phrenology (फ्रेनॉलजि)	– मस्तिष्कशास्त्र
pia matter (पाया मॅटर)	– मृदू आवरण
pon (पॉन)	– सेतू
peripheral nervous system (पेरिफेरल नर्व्हस सिस्टम)	– सीमावर्ती/परिसरीय नससंख्या
prefontal lobotomy (प्रीफ्रंटल लोबोटॉमी)	– अग्रखंड विभक्तीकरण शस्त्रक्रिया
proprioceptors (प्रोप्रिओसेप्टर्स)	– आंतरेंद्रिय ग्राहक
prosopagnosia (प्रोसोपॅग्नेशिया)	– प्रत्यभिज्ञाअक्षमता
receptor (रिसेप्टर)	– ग्राहकपेशी
reflex (रिफ्लेक्स)	– प्रतिक्षिप्त क्रिया
reticular formation (रेटिक्युलर फॉर्मेशन)	– जालरचना बंध

sensation (सेन्सेशन)	- वेदन
sleep centre (स्लीप सेंटर)	- निद्राकेंद्र
somatic nervous system (सोमॅटिक नर्व्हस सिस्टम)	- कायिक नससंस्था
somato sensory area (सोमॅटोसेन्सरी एरिया)	- कायिकवेदन क्षेत्र
speech centre (स्पीच सेंटर)	- वाचाकेंद्र
spinal cord (स्पायनल कॉर्ड)	- मज्जारज्जू
split brain (स्प्लिट ब्रेन)	- विभक्त मेंदू गोलार्ध
squid magnotomy (स्किड मॅग्नोटॉमी)	- स्किड-स्कॅन
stereotactic neurosurgery (स्टिरिओटॅक्टिक न्यूरोसर्जरी)	- मेंदूक्षेत्रवेधी मानसशस्त्रक्रिया
subcortical (सबकॉर्टिकल)	- मेंदूदृष्ठाखालील अग्रभाग
synaesthesia (सायनिस्थेशिया)	- इंद्रियवेदनांतर
synapse (सिनॅप्स)	- नसबंध
testosterone (टेस्टोस्टेरॉन)	- पुरुष लैंगिक ग्रंथीस्राव
trepanning (ट्रेपनिंग)	- कवटीस छिद्र पाडणे
thalamus (थलॅमस)	- चेताक्षेपक
temporal lobe (टेंपोरल लोंब)	- कुंभखंड
visual cortex (व्हिजुअल कॉर्टेक्स)	- मेंदूपृष्ठावरील दृष्टिकेंद्र
Wernicke's area (वेर्निक्स एरिया)	- वेर्निक भाषाकेंद्र

परिशिष्ट ४
संख्याशास्त्रीय शब्दावली
(Terms releted to Statistics)

bell-shaped curve (बेल शेप्ड् कर्व्ह)	-	घंटाकार वक्र
bimodal distribution (बायमोडल डिस्ट्रिब्युशन)	-	द्विशिखरी वितरण
central tendency (सेंट्रल टेंडन्सी)	-	केंद्रीय प्रवृत्ती
critical Value (क्रिटिकल व्हॅल्यू)	-	निर्णयात्मक मूल्य
descriptive statistics (डिस्क्रिप्टिव्ह स्टॅटिस्टिक्स्)	-	वर्णनात्मक संख्याशास्त्र
frequency (फ्रिक्वेन्सी)	-	वारंवारता
frequency distribution (फ्रिक्वेन्सी डिस्ट्रिब्युशन)	-	वारंवारता वितरण/विभाजन
frequency polygone (फ्रिक्वेन्सी पॉलिगॉन)	-	वारंवारता बहुभुज
Gaussian curve (गोसियन कर्व्ह)	-	सामान्य-वितरण-वक्र
grouping (ग्रुपिंग)	-	प्राप्तांक संघटीकरण
histogram (हिस्टोग्रॅम)	-	स्तंभालेख
inferential statistics (इन्फरेन्शियल स्टॅटिस्टिक्स)	-	अनुमानात्मक संख्याशास्त्र
j-curve (जे-कर्व्ह)	-	'जे' आकाराचा वक्र
level of significance (लेव्हल ऑफ सिग्निफिकन्स)	-	संख्याशास्त्रीय पातळी
mean (मीन)	-	सरासरी
mean-deviation (मीन डेव्हिएशन)	-	सरासरी विचलन
measures of central tendency (मेझर्स ऑफ सेंट्रल टेंडन्सी)	-	केंद्रीय प्रवृत्तीची परिमाणे
median (मिडियन)	-	मध्यांक
mode (मोड)	-	बहुलक
multimodal distribution (मल्टीमोडल डिस्ट्रीब्युशन)	-	बहुशिखरी वितरण
non-parametric statistics (नॉनपॅरॅमेट्रिक स्टॅटिस्टिक्स)	-	मानवी वर्तनसंदर्भातील संख्याशास्त्र/सामान्यवितरणाभावाचे संख्याशास्त्र
norm (नॉर्म)	-	प्रमाणक

normal distribution (नॉर्मल डिस्ट्रिब्युशन)	-	प्रसामान्य वितरण
observed value (आब्सर्व्हड् व्हॅल्यू)	-	निरक्षित अंकात्मक मूल्य
ordinate data (ऑर्डिनेट डेटा)	-	चढत्या श्रेणीचा प्रदत्त
parametic statistics (पॅरॅमेट्रिक स्टॅटिस्टिक्स)	-	प्रसामान्य वितरणाचे संख्याशास्त्र
percentile (पर्सेंटाईल)	-	शततमक
percentile norm (पर्सेंटाईल नॉर्म)	-	शततमक प्रमाणक
predictive statistics (प्रेडिक्टिव्ह स्टॅटिस्टिक्स)	-	भाकितात्मक संख्याशास्त्र
probability (प्रॉबेबिलिटी)	-	संभवनीयता
quartile (क्वार्टाईल)	-	चतुर्थक
quartile deviation (क्वार्टाईल डेव्हिएशन)	-	चतुर्थक विचलन
random sampling (रॅन्डम साम्पलिन्ग)	-	यादृच्छिक नमुना चयन/ अनियत नमुना चयन
range (रेंज)	-	विस्तार
rank-order (रॅंक ऑर्डर)	-	चढती वा उतरती श्रेणी
representative sample (रिप्रेझेंटेटिव्ह सॅंपल)	-	प्रातिनिधिक नमुना गट
sample (सॅंपल)	-	नमुना गट
score (स्कोअर)	-	प्राप्तांक
standard score (स्टॅंडर्ड स्कोअर)	-	प्रमाणित प्राप्तांक
standard deveation (स्टॅंडर्ड डेव्हिएशन)	-	प्रमाण विचलन
statistical infreqnency (स्टॅटिस्टिकल इन्फ्रिक्वेन्सी)	-	संख्याशास्त्रीय दुर्मिळता/ अपसामान्यता
statistical significance (स्टॅटिस्टिकल सिग्निफिकन्स)	-	संख्याशास्त्रीय लक्षणीयता
stratified sample (स्ट्रॅटिफाईड सॅंपल)	-	स्तरीय नमुना
test of difference (टेस्ट ऑफ डिफरन्स)	-	लक्षणीय भिन्नतेची कसोटी
t-test (टी-टेस्ट)	-	सरासरींमधील लक्षणीय भिन्नतेची कसोटी
varience (व्हेरियन्स)	-	प्रमाण विचलनाचा वर्ग

परिशिष्ट ५

(काही विदेशी व भारतीय नामवंत मानसशास्त्रज्ञ व मानसशास्त्रासाठी वेदन-
संवेदन, नससंस्था, व्यक्तिमत्त्व, बुद्धिमत्ता, स्मृती, बोधावस्था इ. अनेकविध
क्षेत्रात - योगदान देणाऱ्या महनीय व्यक्ती)

Adler, Alfred (ॲडलर ऑल्फ्रेड)

Allport G.W. (ऑलपोर्ट जी. डब्ल्यू.)

Alzheimer Alois (अल्झायमर अलॉइस)

Anderson J.R. (अँडरसन जे. आर्.)

Aristotle (ॲरिस्टॉटल)

Asch, Solomon (ॲश सॉलोमन)

Atkinson J.W. (ॲटकिन्सन जे. डब्ल्यू.)

Bandura Albert (बांदुरा अल्बर्ट)

Bakdley Allen (बॅडली ॲलन)

Bard, Philip (बार्ड- फिलिप)

Barron F. X. (बॅरन एफ्. एक्स.)

Bekhterev V. M. (बेख्तेरेव्ह व्ही. एम्.)

Benson Herbert (बेन्सन हर्बर्ट)

Berger Hans (बर्गर हान्स)

Berne Eric (बर्न एरिक)

Bernreuter R. G. (बर्नरुटर आर्. जी.)

Bernstein Basil (बर्नस्टीन बेसिल)

Binet, Alfred (बिने ऑल्फ्रेड)

Bleuler Eugen (ब्ल्युलर यूजेन)

Boring E. G. (बोरिंग इ. जी.)

Bose Girindra (बोस गिरिंद्र)

Braid James (ब्रेड जेम्स)

Broca Paul (ब्रोका पॉल)

Bruner J. S. (ब्रुनर जे. एस्.)

Cajal Santiago (काजल सँटिॲगो)

Cannon W. B. (कॅनन डब्ल्यू. बी.)

Cattell R. B. (कॅटेल आर्. बी.)

Charcot J. M. (चॉरकॉट जे. एम्.)

Chomsky A. N. (चॉम्स्की ए. एन्.)

Conrad (कोनरॅड)

Costa / Mcray (कोस्टा / मॅक्रे)

Craick / Lockhart (क्रेक / लॉकहार्ट)

Darwin Charles (डार्विन चार्ल्स)

Dement (डीमेंट)

Descartes Rene' (डेकार्ट रेनी)

Dewey John (ड्यूई जॉन)

Dr. Jina S.P.K (जीना एस्. पी. के.)

Ebbinghaus H. V. (एबिंगहॉस एच्. व्ही.)

Ekman Paul (एकमन पॉल)

Ellis Albert (एलिस अलबर्ट)

Erikson Erik H. (एरिक्सन एरिक एच्.)

Eysenck H. J. (आयझेंक एच्. जे.)

Fechner G. T. (फेकनर जी. टी.)

Feldman Robert (फेल्डमन रॉबर्ट)

Freeman Joan (फ्रीमन जोन)

Freud Anna (फ्रॉईड ॲना)

Freud Sigmond (फ्रॉईड सिगमंड)

Fromm Erich (फ्रॉम एरिक)

Galton Francis (गाल्टन फ्रॉन्सिस)
Goldberg (गोल्डबर्ग)
Goldstein Kurt (गोल्डस्टीन कुर्त)
Golman Daniel (गोलमन डॅनियल)
Gopalswami M.V. (गोपालस्वामी एम्. व्ही.)
Gregory R. L. (ग्रेगरी आर्. एल्.)
Guildford J. P. (गिल्डफर्ड जे. पी.)

Hall G. S. (हॉल. जी. एस्)
Harlow Harry (हार्लों हॅरी)
Hebb D. O. (हेब डी. ओ.)
Helmholts H. L. (हेल्महोल्ट्झ एच्. एल्.)
Hillgard E. R. (हिलगार्ड इ. आर्.)
Horney Karen (हॉर्नी कॅरेन)
Hull C. L. (हल् सी. एल्.)
Huseman (ह्यूजमन)

Ishihara Shinobu (इशिहारा शिनोबू)

James William (जेम्स विल्यम्)
Jung C. G. (जंग सी. जी.)

Kakkar S (कंक्कर एस्.)
Kamphus (कॅंफस)
Kant Emanuel (कांट इम्यॅन्युअल)
Keller Fredrick (केलर फ्रेड्रिक)
Kleine Willi (क्लाईन विली)
Kleinfelter H. F. (क्लाइन फेल्टर एच्. एफ्.)
Koffka kurt (कॉफ्का कुर्त)

Kohler wolfgang (कोहलर वुल्फगॅंग)
Korsakoff S. S. (कोर्साकॉफ एस्. एस्.)
Kretschmer Ernst (क्रेशमर अन्स्र्ट)
Kuder G. F. (कूडर जी. एफ्.)

Lange Carl G. (लँग कार्ल जी.)
Lewin Kurt (लेविन कुर्त)
Likert Rensis (लायकर्ट रेन्सिस)
Lorenz Konrad (लोरेंझ कॉनरॅड)
Luria A. R. (ल्यूरिया ए. आर्.)

Maharshi Mahesh Yogi (महर्षी महेश योगी)
Maiti H.P. (मैती एच्. पी.)
Maslow A. H. (मॅस्लो ए. एच्.)
Matarzzo (मटार्झो)
Mayer (मेयर)
Mc Dougall William (मॅक्डुगल विल्यम्)
Mc Lelland David (मॅक्लीलँड डेव्हिड)
Mead Margaret (मीड मागरिट)
Mendel G. (मेंडेल जी.)
Merril M.A. (मेरिल एम्. ए.)
Mesmer Franz A. (मेस्मेर फ्रॉंझ ए.)
Miller G. A. (मिलर जी. ए.)
Mishra G. (मिश्रा जी.)
Mohsin S.M. (मोहसीन एस्. एम्.)
Moreno J. L. (मोरेनो जे. एल्.)
Moris C. G. (मॉरिस सी. जी.)
Moro Ernst (मोरो अन्स्र्ट)
Morton John (मॉर्टन जॉन)

Muller Johannes (म्युलर जोहनीज)
Muller-Lyer F. K. (म्युलर-लायर एफ़. के.)
Murphy Gardner (मर्फी गार्डनर)
Murray H. A. (मरे एच्. ए.)
Nandy A. (नंदी ए.)

Neisser Murray H. A. (निस्सेर मरे यू. आर्)
Newport Ellissa (न्यूपोर्ट एलिसा)

Oden Gregg (ओडेन ग्रेग)
Osgood C. E. (ऑसगुड सी. इ.)

Pandey J. (पांडे जे.)
Paranjape A. C. (परांजपे ए. सी.)
Parik U. (परिक यू.)
Patanjali (पंतजली)
Pavlov Ivan (पाव्हलॉव्ह इव्हॅन)
Pavlov Jean (पॅहलोर जीन)
Piaget Jean (पियाजे जीन)
Plato (प्लेटो)
Prabhu P. H. (प्रभु पी. एच्.)

Rao Ramchandra (राव रामचंद्र)
Rogers Carl (रॉजर्स कार्ल)
Rhine J. B. (न्हाईन जे. बी.)
Robinson F. P. (रॉबिन्सन एफ़. पी.)
Rorschach Hermann (रोर्शाक् हर्मन)
Rosenthal R. (रोझेंथॉल आर्.)
Rumelhart (रुमेलहार्ट)
Ryle Gilbert (राईल गिल्बर्ट)

Schacter Daniel (शॅक्टर डॅनियल)
Schroeder (प्रोडर)
Seashosre C. L. (सीझोअर सी. एल्.)
Seligman M.E.P. (सेलिगमन एम. इ. पी.)
Sengupta N. N. (सेनगुप्ता एन्. एन्.)
Seyal Brajendranath (सियल ब्रजेंद्रनाथ)
Sheldon W. H. (शेल्डन डब्ल्यू. एच.)
Shiffrin (शिफ्रीन)
Siman Theodore (सायमन थिओडोर)
Singer Jerom (सिंगर जेरॉम)
Sinha D (सिन्हा डी.)
Sinha J. B. P. (सिन्हा जे. बी. पी.)
Skinner B. F. (स्किअर बी. एफ़.)
Spearman C. E. (स्पिअरमन सी. इ.)
Spery Roger (स्पेरी रॉजर)
Stern Wilhelm (स्टर्न विल्हेल्म)
Sternberg S. (स्टर्नबर्ग एस्.)
Strong E.K. (स्ट्रॉंग इ. के.)

Terman L. M. (टर्मन एल्. एम्.)
Thorndike E. L. (थॉर्नडिक् इ. एल्.)
Thurstone L. L. (थर्स्टन एल्. एल्.)
Titchner E. B.s (टिचनेर इ. बी.)
Toffler Allen (टॉफलर ऑलन)
Tolman E. C. (टोलमन इ. सी.)
Tripathi R. (त्रिपाठी आर.)
Tulving (टुलविंग)

Vygotsky L.S. (व्हिगोटस्की एल्. एस्)

Wagner Allan (वॅगनर ऑलन)

Watson J. B. (वॉटसन जे. बी.)

Weber E. H. (वेबर इ. एच्.)

Wechsler David (वेश्लर डेव्हिड)

Wernicke Carl (वेर्निक कार्ल)

Wertheimer Max (वर्दायमर मॅक्स)

Whiten Kalkins (व्हाईटन कॉल्किन्स)

Woodworth R. S. (वुडवर्थ आर. एस्)

Wundt W. M. (वुन्ट् डब्ल्यू. एम्.)

Yerkes Robert M. (यर्कस् रॉबर्ट एम्.)

Zeigarnik Bluma (झायगर्निक ब्ल्यूमा)

Zollner J. K. E. (झोलनर जे. के. एफ्.)

संदर्भ ग्रंथ

1) Dictionary of Psychology IInd ed.
   Published by Penguin Group 1195 - by Arthur S. Reber.
2) A student's Dictionary of Psychology
   Published by Psychology Press - Taylor & Francis Group
   Indian Reprint 2003 - by David A Statt.
3) A comprehinsive Dictionary of Psychology
   Published by Abhishek Publications Chandigarh 2004. ed &
   compiled by John D. Grand.
4) Anmol's Dictionary of Psychology
   by Anmol Publication Pvt. Ltd. New Delhi Reprint 2006
   by Sharma & Bhatia.
5) मानसशास्त्र – अनु. प्रा. अमृता ओक, प्रा. शोभना अभ्यंकर,.
   प्रा.शीला गोविलकर, दक्षिण आशिया आवृत्ती ०८. पिअर्सन एज्युकेशन, दिल्ली
6) आधुनिक सामान्य मानसशास्त्र – २००५, पाटील, इनामदार, गाडेकर
   डायमंड पब्लिकेशन्स, पुणे
7) प्रगत सामाजिक मानसशास्त्र – २००६, पाटील, इनामदार, गाडेकर
   डायमंड पब्लिकेशन्स, पुणे
8) मानसशास्त्र संज्ञा, सिद्धान्त कोश – डॉ. बी. आर. जोशी
   डायमंड पब्लिकेशन्स, पुणे –

लेखक – परिचय

प्रा. मुकुंद इनामदार

- चां. ता. बोरा महाविद्यालय, शिरूर, जि. पुणे येथून मानसशास्त्र, तत्त्वज्ञान विभागप्रमुख म्हणून निवृत्त. मानसशास्त्र विषयाचे प्रदीर्घ अध्यापन (१९७२-२००४)

- महाविद्यालयातर्फे प्रकाशित झालेल्या परिसरातील १०० गावांच्या शैक्षणिक, आधारित 'विकासवेध' या ग्रंथाचे प्रमुख संपादक (१९८७).

- E.M.R.C. पुणे मध्ये Social Avoidance या विषयावर संहितालेखन केले.

- ''विद्यार्थी, पालक व स्थानिक नागरिकांच्या महाविद्यालयीन पदवी शिक्षणाबाबतच्या अभिवृत्ती'' या विषयावरील विद्यापीठ अनुदान आयोगाने मंजूर केलेला लघुशोध प्रकल्प पूर्ण करून 'नॅक'च्या मार्गदर्शक सूचनेप्रमाणे महाविद्यालयाचे स्वयंमूल्यमापन केले. (२०००-२००१).

- स्वाध्याय संस्कारमाला-भाग १ (मृत्युंजय प्रकाशन, पुणे) या ग्रंथाचे सहलेखन १९७१.

- आधुनिक सामान्य मानसशास्त्र, (डायमंड पब्लिकेशन्स, पुणे २००५)

- प्रगत सामाजिक मानसशास्त्र, (डायमंड पब्लिकेशन्स, पुणे २००६)

.

www.ingramcontent.com/pod-product-compliance
Lightning Source LLC
Chambersburg PA
CBHW060902280326
41934CB00007B/1153